ALSO AVAILABLE IN THE SERIES

A to Z Great Modern Artists

£14.99
978 1 84403 780 3

A lively, visually stunning introduction to the world of modern artists, from Albers to Zox, via Basquiat, Kahlo, Warhol and more.

A to Z Great Film Directors

£14.99
978 1 84403 822 0

An accessible yet highly informative introduction to 52 of the world's greatest film directors, from Almodóvar to Zhang Yimou, by way of Campion, Fellini, Scorsese, Lee and more.

A TO Z GREAT MODERN WRITERS

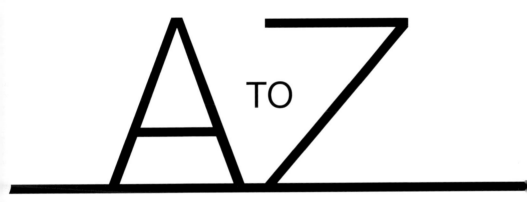

A TO Z GREAT MODERN WRITERS
ANDY TUOHY

WITH TEXT BY CAROLINE TAGGART

CASSELL
ILLUSTRATED

An Hachette UK Company
www.hachette.co.uk

First published in Great Britain in 2017 by Cassell, a division of Octopus Publishing Group Ltd,
Carmelite House, 50 Victoria Embankment, London EC4Y 0DZ
www.octopusbooks.co.uk

Distributed in the US by Hachette Book Group,
1290 Avenue of the Americas , 4th and 5th Floors, New York, NY 10020

Distributed in Canada by Canadian Manda Group,
664 Annette St.Toronto, Ontario, Canada M6S 2C8

ISBN 978 1 84403 913 5

A CIP catalogue record for this book is available from the British Library.

Printed and bound in China

10 9 8 7 6 5 4 3 2 1

Commissioning Editor Hannah Knowles
Senior Editor Pauline Bache
Designer Andy Tuohy
Junior Designer (for Octopus) Jack Storey
Picture Library Manager Jennifer Veall
Production Controller Meskerem Berhane

CONTENTS

PREFACE

When I produced books of *Great Modern Artists* and *Great Film Directors* a couple of years ago, I fretted about how to reduce the list of entries to the required length. It's been even more difficult with *Great Modern Writers* and frankly, it would have easier to produce 520 names than 52. Caroline Taggart, our editor Hannah Knowles and I started by defining 'modern', very roughly, as 'flourishing in the 20th century'. The oldest writer here is Proust, born in 1871; the youngest Ishiguro, born in 1954. So no Hardy, no Conrad, no H G Wells. We also insisted that our writers had been around long enough to show that they would have a lasting influence: that they would still be read decades if not centuries on. That meant leaving out contemporary stars such as Hilary Mantel and Alan Hollinghurst, both of whom would almost certainly make the cut if we were to revise this book in ten years' time. And we wanted to make our list as 'inclusive' as possible, in terms of both international scope and of not being dominated by straight white men.

There are some names here that I'm sure no one would argue with – Atwood, Camus, Joyce, Updike – and some that are more contentious. That's partly because I wanted the subjects to be graphically interesting. You may argue that Haruki Murakami would have been a more worthy representative of Japan than Yukio Mishima, but I was fascinated by Mishima's samurai connections and extravagant personality. I also wanted to include some personal favourites – hence Philip K Dick and Aleksandr Solzhenitsyn.

My ideas sent Caroline to read new authors and ones she hadn't read for years; her enthusiasm inspired me to do the same and we were excited by Zora Neale Hurston and Clarice Lispector, new to both of us. But I was pleased to find how many authors I *was* familiar with, even if I hadn't read Ford Madox Ford since school.

The 'works to read' are suggestions only: there were times (notably with Gabriel García Márquez and Graham Greene) when reducing the list to five was a real struggle, so the book is a jumping-off point. My son was born when I was working on the previous *A to Z*s: he's three now, and I'm looking forward to introducing him to these authors (though perhaps not D H Lawrence just yet). I hope you too will find old friends, forgotten passions and new acquaintances.

Andy Tuohy

A

TO

C

ACHEBE
ANGELOU
ATWOOD
BALDWIN
de BEAUVOIR
BECKETT
BORGES
CALVINO
CAMUS
CAREY
CARTER

CHINUA ACHEBE

NIGERIAN
1930–2013

It is hard, in the 21st century, to imagine a time – little more than 50 years ago – when the English establishment believed that the English language could express only English ideas. It was partly to dispute this that Chinua Achebe chose to write his seminal novel, *Things Fall Apart* (1958), in English rather than in his native Igbo. But he wrote in a particular kind of English, one that a Nigerian reader would recognize as the way Nigerians spoke. In so doing, he showed that an African writer could adopt English and make it his (or her) own. He also, on a continent that boasted many indigenous tongues, chose a language that was familiar to vast numbers of people.

Things Fall Apart is, quite simply, the first great African novel written by an African. As such, it was and is of monumental importance. It was written at a time when Nigeria, along with much of the rest of Africa, wase emerging from the colonial era into independence, and Africans across the continent were experiencing a crisis of transition. In rebuttal of the disparaging view of Africa portrayed in the novels of Europeans such as Joseph Conrad and Joyce Cary, Achebe wanted to give his people a sense of identity and emphasize that African civilizations and cultures had existed and flourished before the arrival of the Europeans.

The novel's setting is the Igbo village of Umuofia, where the warrior Okonkwo – a powerful but flawed figure who has been likened to a Shakespearean tragic hero –

WORKS TO READ

- *Things Fall Apart* (1958) and the other two in the *African* trilogy: *No Longer at Ease* (1960) and *Arrow of God* (1964)
- *A Man of the People* (1966)
- *Anthills of the Savannah* (1987)
- *Hopes and Impediments: Selected Essays 1965–87* (1988)
- *Collected Poems* (2005)

DID YOU KNOW?

Things Fall Apart almost never made it into print. Achebe posted the only handwritten copy of the book from Nigeria to a typing agency in London, where it languished until his boss at the Nigerian Broadcasting House Service, Mrs Beattie, went in person to London and demanded a copy be typed.

lives in fear of failure and weakness and is unable to cope with the changes that are threatening the way he looks at the world. Chief among these is the arrival of Christian missionaries, the first of whom is gentle and conciliatory, respectful of the values of the people he has come to convert, while the second is uncompromising and confrontational in a way that inevitably leads to violence and tragedy.

Achebe in 1970

Achebe followed *Things Fall Apart* with two further novels, in what has become known as *The African Trilogy: No Longer at Ease* (1960) shows Okonkwo's English-educated grandson clashing with the ruling elite in Nigeria, while *Arrow of God* (1964) focuses on a local priest's battles with the missionaries.

Achebe himself was brought up as a Christian and went to a prestigious Nigerian university, yet he retained an understanding and esteem for the pagan way of life; its oral tradition had been an important part of his childhood and had nurtured his love of language. *Things Fall Apart* is full of the proverbs, stories and legends that had been passed from generation to generation. 'Proverbs', Achebe said, 'are the palm oil with which words are eaten'.

50th Anniversary Edition

THINGS FALL APART

Chinua Achebe

Things Fall Apart, 1958

MAYA
ANGELOU

AMERICAN
1928–2014

Maya Angelou's first volume of autobiography, *I Know Why the Caged Bird Sings* (1969), took the world by storm and became the first-ever bestselling book by a black woman. It was seen as a significant breakthrough for all women writers, whatever their ethnic origins.

It's a memoir of her childhood in the segregated town of Stamps, Arkansas, where she and her brother, Bailey, were brought up by their strong-minded and religious grandmother, who ran the general store. From outside the store, white plantation-owners would collect black cotton-pickers at dawn and return them, dog-tired and downtrodden, at dusk. On Saturdays, Angelou reminisced later in life, the black people would gather to socialize in the store and they would be 'sassy'; it was only when a white person appeared that they would assume the meekness she described as 'the mask'. As a small child Angelou fantasized about being white, 'so that I wouldn't be looked at with such loathing'; and when she returned to Stamps in 1982 to make a documentary about her life, she was still unwilling to cross the railroad tracks to the white side of town, because of the evil memories it would awaken.

Raped by her mother's lover at the age of seven, Angelou became convinced that her voice had later been responsible for the man's death; as a result, for several years she refused, or felt unable, to speak, except to her brother. The influence of a local

WORKS TO READ

- *I Know Why the Caged Bird Sings* (1969)
- *Just Give Me a Cool Drink of Water 'fore I Diiie* (poetry, 1971)
- *Gather Together in My Name* (1974)
- *And Still I Rise* (poetry, 1978)
- *Singin' and Swingin' and Gettin' Merry Like Christmas* (1976)
- *The Heart of a Woman* (1981)

DID YOU KNOW?

Maya Angelou was probably the first black person to be employed as a streetcar conductor in San Francisco. She sat at the transit office for two weeks until they gave her the job, which she later said she wanted because she liked the uniforms and liked working with people.

woman, who encouraged her to read aloud and to recognize poetry as 'music for the human voice', eventually helped her to overcome this trauma.

In her 30s she worked as an actress, dancer and singer, then became involved with the civil rights movement, working closely with both Malcolm X and Martin Luther King, Jr. It was after these two men were assassinated (in 1965 and 1968 respectively) that she began writing seriously. She also became an academic, teaching American Studies at Wake Forest University in North Carolina. She advocated not Feminism but 'womanism', a quality she felt was embodied in black women and included the strength, love and humour that she had observed in the women around her during her childhood. She produced six further volumes of autobiography, every bit as frank as *I Know Why the Caged Bird Sings*. The first two of these – *Gather Together in My Name* (1974) and *Singin' and Swingin' and Gettin' Merry Like Christmas* (1976) – focus on her experiences as a young single mother and the perpetual struggles of a black woman against all sorts of prejudice.

Angelou was also a prolific poet and author of children's books. The many recordings of her performing her own poetry ('reciting' would be too bland a word) show her rich, warm, passionate voice bringing her work to life as no other reader could.

I Know Why the Caged Bird Sings, 1969

Angelou posing for the cover of her album, *Miss Calypso*, 1957

17

MARGARET
ATWOOD

CANADIAN
BORN 1939

With many authors, you pick up their new book knowing roughly what to expect. Not so with Canada's foremost female novelist, short-story writer and poet. Her novels range from a comic romp about a woman who fakes her own death so that she can run away from her absurdly complicated life (*Lady Oracle*, 1976) to the magical realism of *The Robber Bride* (1993), in which three women encounter an old friend they had believed dead, and find that she has had an affair with all their husbands (but does she really exist?). There's true crime in *Alias Grace* (1996), about a woman convicted of murder in 19th-century Canada; a post-modern 'novel within a novel within a novel' in *The Blind Assassin* (2000); and a reworking of Homer's *Odyssey* in *The Penelopiad* (2005). Common – indeed, defining – features are strong female protagonists and, often, a setting in Atwood's native Ontario.

That said, Atwood is probably best known for her 'speculative fiction', featuring her sometimes gloomy but still life-affirming views of the not-so-distant future. In *The Handmaid's Tale* (1985) lower-caste women bear children for members of the elite, while the *MaddAddam* trilogy – *Oryx and Crake* (2003), *The Year of the Flood* (2009) and *MaddAddam* (2013) – follows the outcome of an environmental meltdown that wipes out most of the human race. In *The Heart Goes Last* (2015) the meltdown has been a financial one, with job opportunities now being created through a

WORKS TO READ

- *The Handmaid's Tale* (1985)
- *The Robber Bride* (1993)
- *Alias Grace* (1996)
- *The Blind Assassin* (2000)
- *The Heart Goes Last* (2015)

DID YOU KNOW?

In 1987 Margaret Atwood published the fundraising cook book, *CanLit Foodbook*. At the time, she said to CBC News 'Canadian literature is rolling in food, a lot of it fish'. You can find Atwood's Baked Lemon Custard Pie recipe on the online magazine, *Bon Appétit*, where it's currently rated 3.5 out of 4 by Epicurious reviews.

for-profit penal system, which means that there is a constant need for prisoners to keep the prisons full.

Atwood has described speculative fiction as 'when you are just ahead of reality but sometimes reality is just ahead of you…By the time I got to the third book [of the *MaddAddam* trilogy], reality had caught up with the first one in quite a few of the instances…so this is not twisted old Margaret making this stuff up.'

Speculative fiction, she says, 'allows you to take things to their next logical conclusion step'. If she's right, be warned – the sex robots she describes in *The Heart Goes Last* could be the next big thing.

66

When things are really dismal, you can laugh, or you can cave in completely.

99

Atwood at the Edinburgh International Book Festival in August 2005

The
Heart
Goes
Last

Margaret
ATWOOD

BLOOMSBURY

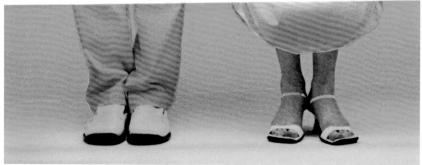

The Heart Goes Last, 2015

JAMES
BALDWIN

AMERICAN
1924–87

At the tender age of 14 James Baldwin became a preacher in Harlem, New York City, in part, he later realized, to escape the dangers of being a proud, strong-willed, black man in the US at that time. When he was 17 he left the church, having begun to see that he was 'hiding behind the pulpit'. Like the heroine Margaret in his play *The Amen Corner* (1954), Baldwin discovered that he was using faith as a way of avoiding the terrors and responsibilities of love and life. One of the things he was hiding from was his own homosexuality.

In 1948, increasingly angry at the hostility with which black people were treated, he moved to Paris. There, he would have the freedom to become a writer, not just a 'black writer'. 'If you're not French in France, you simply don't exist,' he later recalled. 'I was invisible in France and that was what I needed.'

A few years later he became seriously ill and was taken to stay in the Swiss Alps to recuperate. He took with him his typewriter and two records. Listening to these records – the music of Bessie Smith and Fats Waller – is what gave him 'the key to the language' that he needed to complete his first novel, *Go Tell It on the Mountain* (1953), based on his experiences as a young preacher in Harlem.

Issues of race pervade much of Baldwin's work, and from an early stage he was an outspoken supporter of the civil rights movement. But these themes are noticeably

WORKS TO READ

- *Go Tell It on the Mountain* (1953)
- *Notes of a Native Son* (1955)
- *Giovanni's Room* (1956)
- *The Fire Next Time* (1963)
- *Going to Meet the Man* (short stories, 1965)
- *No Name in the Street* (essays, 1972)

DID YOU KNOW?

Along with approximately 10 per cent of the global population, Baldwin was left-handed. In his writing hand he suffered mild arthritis, with more frequency when the weather was wet and humid. Regardless of the arthritis, he never typed, and always preferred to write in long-hand.

absent from his best-known novel. *Giovanni's Room*, published in 1956, when homosexuality was still illegal in the US, centres on a passionate gay love affair and was, for its time, shockingly explicit. Yet Baldwin maintained that the book was not about homosexuality per se; it was, like much of his work, about loneliness and 'what happens when you're afraid to love anybody'. It is, however, not insignificant that the central character, David, is a white American Protestant, who behaves despicably and destructively rather than face up to the challenges demanded by love.

In addition to writing novels, plays and short stories, Baldwin was an essayist of great power and invention. *Notes of a Native Son* (1955), a collection written when he was only in his 20s, shows him at his most unabashed, his most vocal, in his investigation of what it means to be black and American.

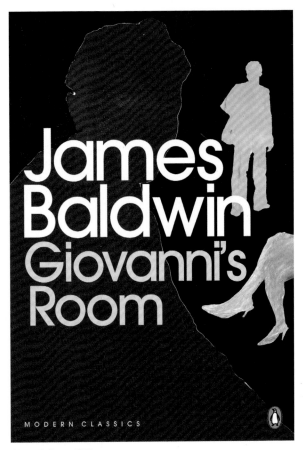

Giovanni's Room, 1956

Baldwin demonstrating in Paris in support of the March on Washington, August 1963

SIMONE
de BEAUVOIR

FRENCH
1908–86

There had been 'feminist writers' before Simone de Beauvoir, but she was perhaps the first to take the concept of male domination by the throat and shake it until it rattled. In her massive and ground-breaking work *The Second Sex* (1949), she took the view that men imposed on women an ideal of femininity, and that both sexes were then disappointed when women didn't measure up. She also made a distinction between a female human being (one who happened to possess a womb) and a woman, with all the cultural and emotional baggage that that entailed. She wrote frankly about sex (inside and outside marriage), orgasm, lesbianism, contraception and abortion, and criticized the institution of marriage itself. This was heady stuff in hungry post-war Paris, just five years after French women had been given the vote.

Supremely intelligent, de Beauvoir was born into a repressive Catholic family from which education seemed her only escape. She met Jean-Paul SARTRE while studying at the Sorbonne and graduated second in their class, behind him. They became lifelong (though frequently unfaithful) lovers and intellectual partners, working together on his magazine *Les Temps Modernes*, and achieving celebrity in philosophical and literary circles.

While Sartre had, according to de Beauvoir, the intellect of a great philosopher, she saw herself as primarily a creative writer. Her first novel, *She Came to Stay* (1943), is a

WORKS TO READ
- *She Came to Stay* (1943)
- *The Blood of Others* (1945)
- *The Ethics of Ambiguity* (non-fiction, 1947)
- *The Second Sex* (non-fiction, 1949)
- *The Mandarins* (1954)

DID YOU KNOW?
Simone de Beauvoir never had children and never married. At her funeral around 5,000 mourners gathered to pay tribute to the woman thought of as the mother of the modern women's movement. She is now buried alongside Sartre in Montparnasse Cemetery.

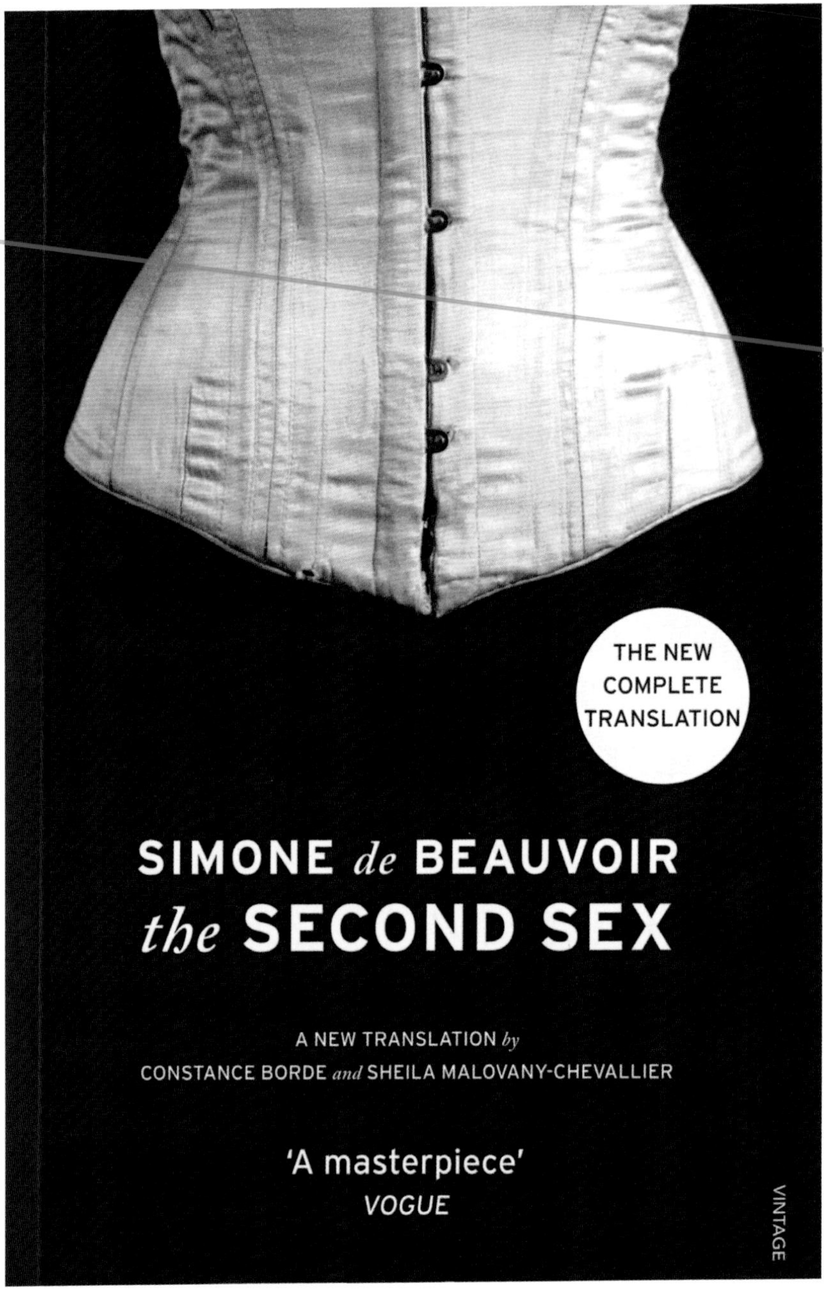

THE NEW
COMPLETE
TRANSLATION

SIMONE *de* BEAUVOIR
the SECOND SEX

A NEW TRANSLATION *by*
CONSTANCE BORDE *and* SHEILA MALOVANY-CHEVALLIER

'A masterpiece'
VOGUE

VINTAGE

The Second Sex, 1949

thinly veiled account of the angst-ridden *ménage à quatre* that she and Sartre shared with two much younger women. She also drew closely on her own life for her novel *The Mandarins* (1954), which won her the prestigious Prix Goncourt for 'the best and most imaginative prose work of the year'. The three central characters, under fictitious names, are herself, Sartre and Albert CAMUS, a former close friend with whom Sartre had by this time fallen out; the book's theme is the role of the intellectual in modern society and politics.

Existentialist philosophy is never far from de Beauvoir's work: the novel *The Blood of Others* (1945), set against a background of the French Resistance, discusses the moral responsibilities and choices that the existentialist concept of freedom brings with it; while the essay *The Ethics of Ambiguity* (1947) analyses these ideas and concludes that an individual can be free only if others are free too. It is still regarded as a great and accessible introduction to existentialism 70 years on.

De Beauvoir at her desk in 1953

SAMUEL BECKETT

IRISH
1906–89

Walking home one night in Paris, Samuel Beckett was stabbed by a beggar to whom he had refused to give money. Visiting the man later in prison, Beckett asked why he had done it. '*Je ne sais pas, monsieur,*' came the reply. '*Je m'excuse.*' ('I don't know, sir. I'm sorry.')

It has been said that this is just what Beckett would have responded to any question about human motivation. His works are full of characters who live in dustbins (*Endgame*, 1957), are buried up to their necks in earth (*Happy Days*, 1961) or are interrogating an unseen suspect for no apparent reason (*What Where*, 1983). In his novel *Molloy* (1951) there is a long, hilarious and obsessive-compulsive account of a man on a beach, collecting stones to suck and carefully distributing them between pockets. Why? *Je ne sais pas. Je m'excuse.*

Beckett was born into a middle-class Irish Protestant family, but escaped its restrictions as soon as he could and settled in Paris in the late 1930s. From 1946 he wrote largely in French, which he found more conducive to the simple, pared-down style he was trying to achieve.

Beckett had published poems, essays, reviews and novels before achieving fame with the play *Waiting for Godot* (1952). In it, two tramps are waiting (we don't know why) for Godot (we don't know who he is). They've had their instructions (we don't

WORKS TO READ
- *Molloy* (1951)
- *Waiting for Godot* (play, 1952)
- *Endgame* (play, 1957)
- *Happy Days* (play, 1961)
- *Krapp's Last Tape* (play, 1958)

DID YOU KNOW?
As a representative of Dublin University in two cricket matches against Northamptonshire in 1925 and 1926, Beckett conceded 64 runs without taking a wicket and scored 35 runs in his four innings. He is the only Nobel laureate to have played first-class cricket and he never lost his interest in the sport.

know from whom): they are to wait. At the end of each act, there having been no sign of Godot, one says to the other, 'Well, shall we go?' The other replies, 'Yes, let's go.' The closing stage direction reads, 'They do not move.' *Waiting for Godot* is one of the most important plays of the Theatre of the Absurd – funny, yes, but unsettling and pessimistic, showing the pointlessness of human endeavour.

Equally pointlessly, it would appear, in *Krapp's Last Tape* (1958), a shabby old man listens to recordings of his younger self. As he munches on bananas that he takes from a locked drawer in a desk, the audience learns that, despite his youthful arrogance, he has accomplished nothing. His name has not been chosen at random.

In 1969 Beckett was awarded the Nobel Prize in Literature 'for his writing, which – in new forms for the novel and drama – in the destitution of modern man acquires its elevation'. Later in life, Beckett wrote for television, with increasing emphasis on visual effects: in *Quad* (1981) four characters in different-coloured robes walk silently across the stage in symmetrical patterns. Some of his late stage plays last only a few minutes. 'My last work', he said, 'will be a blank piece of paper.'

Did he achieve it? *Je ne sais pas. Je m'excuse.*

John Hurt in *Krapp's Last Tape* in 2006

Jean Martin, Lucien Raimbourg, Pierre Latour and Albert Remey in *Waiting for Godot* in 1956

JORGE LUIS BORGES

ARGENTINIAN
1899–1986

Although he was widely published in his native Argentina from the 1920s, it was only in the early 1960s that a series of awards and honours brought Jorge Luis Borges international fame. 'People started taking me seriously,' he remarked, 'so I had to live up to it.'

Borges seems, however, never to have taken himself very seriously. Throughout his career he enjoyed hoaxing his public: a notable translator, he published, in addition to his legitimate work, stories that he had produced himself but claimed were the rarely read writings of other great authors. *A Universal History of Infamy* (1935), one of the first-ever literary works to be described as magical realism, is a collection of heavily fictionalized accounts of 'true crime' stories.

Even when he is not trying to perpetrate a hoax, Borges's stories and poems abound with mirrors, masks and labyrinths as they explore the nature of reality and duality. In his short story 'The Circular Ruins' (1940) a man attempts, night after night in his dreams, to create every detail of another person – the beating of his heart, the individual strands of his hair – before realizing that he, too, is an illusion, that someone else is dreaming him. In the poem 'Borges and I' (1960) the author describes himself as two people who share tastes and experiences; one of them strolls through the streets of Buenos Aires while the other weaves his tales and poems – 'and which of

WORKS TO READ

- *A Universal History of Infamy* (short stories, 1935)
- *Fictions* (1944) and *Labyrinths* (1962, both collections of short stories)
- *Extraordinary Tales* (1967, in collaboration with his friend Adolfo Bioy Casares)
- *Selected Poems* (1999)

DID YOU KNOW?

As the Miguel Cané Municipal Library had so few books, when Borges worked there in 1938 he was told to catalogue no more than 100 a day, as any more than this would look bad and leave the other staff nothing to do. This left him plenty of time to work on his own writing.

us is writing this page, I don't know'. At the end of 'The Meeting' (1970), a short story about a small boy witnessing a knife fight, the reader is left wondering if it was the men or the knives who were fighting – perhaps the knives will fight again in other hands.

Borges worked as a librarian, but, as an active opponent of President Juan Perón, he resigned after being 'promoted' to a ludicrous post in Buenos Aires market. He was appointed Director of the National Library when Perón was deposed in 1955, by which time Borges was blind. In 'Poem of the Gifts' he wrote – without 'self-pity or reproach' – about the irony of a blind man being given unlimited access to books.

When Perón was restored in 1973, Borges resigned again. He was by now travelling and lecturing widely, but – to the annoyance of many – was never awarded the Nobel Prize. 'Not granting me the Nobel Prize has become a Scandinavian tradition,' he said. 'Since I was born they have not been granting it to me.'

Borges in his office in Buenos Aires, 1973

Labyrinths, 1962

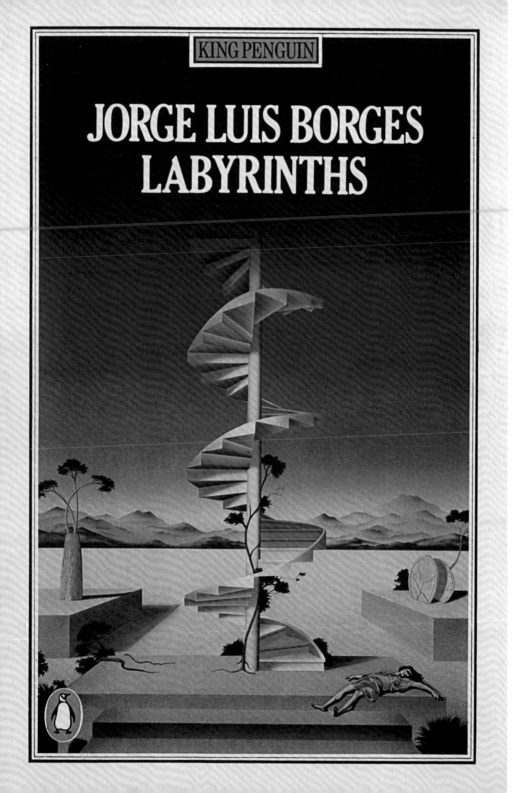

ITALO CALVINO

ITALIAN
1923–85

'You are about to begin reading Italo Calvino's new novel, *If on a winter's night a traveler*. Relax. Concentrate. Dispel every other thought. Let the world around you fade.'

So begins Calvino's most famous work, and the first chapter continues to address you, the reader directly: considering the most comfortable positions for reading, the reasons you have chosen this book, the way you set about reading it. After seven or eight pages you reach the winter's night and the traveller – in a station café that is about to close, carrying a suitcase that he is meant to exchange with a man who has not yet turned up. What the case contains you never learn, because you discover that you are reading a faulty copy. The section you have just finished is repeated again and again; you cannot get beyond the opening pages. You go back to the bookshop to complain and are given a replacement copy – which turns out to be another book entirely.

And so it continues – through ten completely different part-novels and many elusive encounters between yourself and a second, female reader.

Sounds daft? Perhaps it is. But it is also an engrossing take on the importance of reading, the purpose of reading, the difference between truth and fiction, between an original and a fake, and whether or not a novel has to have a hero and heroine who either die or live happily ever after.

WORKS TO READ
- *The Path to the Nest of Spiders* (1947)
- *Italian Folktales* (collection, 1956)
- *The Baron in the Trees* (1957)
- *If on a Winter's Night a Traveler* (1979)
- *Mr Palomar* (1983)

DID YOU KNOW?
Anti-Fascist Calvino refused military service and, at his mother's encouragement, joined the Italian Resistance in 1944. As a result of this, Calvino's parents were arrested and held hostage by the Nazis and his father was almost shot dead before his mother's eyes.

Palomar, 1983

The ultimate meaning to which all stories refer has two faces: the continuity of life, the inevitability of death.

If on a Winter's Night a Traveler, 1979

As a young man Calvino joined the left-wing Italian Resistance and based his first novel, *The Path to the Nest of Spiders* (1947), on his wartime experiences. After having written caricatures of the comrades with whom he had shared chestnuts and the fear of death, he was subsequently filled with remorse and regret. In the 1950s and 1960s he turned his attention from realism to fables, using fantasy as 'a way of looking inside ourselves and our problems'. From this point onwards he began to ponder the nature of the novel and, eventually, he wrote *If on a Winter's Night a Traveler* (1979). With its pastiches of many different styles and genres, he saw this not as an epitaph but as a revival, 'a homage to the traditional novel in the style of the new'. To cope with his complicated narrative structure, he drew detailed patterns and schemas: 'I set myself rules,' he said, 'but I don't always respect them. In some way I am always complicating my life.'

In his last work, *Mr Palomar* (1983), the titular protagonist is an obsessive observer; he wants to see and understand things completely, whether it be a single wave in the ocean, the stars in the sky or the moon. 'A nervous man who lives in a frenzied and congested world', he has much in common with his creator, who had chosen to retire to a quiet home in the Tuscan hills, as far from the frenzy of modern life as it was possible to be.

ALBERT CAMUS

FRENCH

1913–60

'Mother died today. Or perhaps yesterday, I don't know.' This frequently quoted opening line of *The Outsider* (1942), known in the US as *The Stranger*, is an apt summary of its author's 'absurdist' philosophy. Human beings are trapped in solitude, detached from the rest of humanity, with the fear of death hanging over them; those who seek meaning and value in life are doomed to disappointment. Meursault, the narrator of *The Outsider*, is the embodiment of this detachment: he kills a stranger for no better reason than that he is troubled by the heat, and then sits calmly through his own trial, refusing to conform to conventional mores by expressing emotions he doesn't feel.

Born in Algeria, Albert Camus lost his father when he was only a few months old and survived a childhood that was plagued by poverty and ill health. He studied philosophy at the University of Algiers, then worked as a journalist and a playwright – his first major literary work was the play *Caligula*, which he began writing in 1938 (though it wasn't published until 1944). During World War II he joined the French Resistance and conceived a lifelong hatred of totalitarianism. His novel *The Plague* (1947) is based on a typhus epidemic that struck Algeria in 1941–2, but it can also be read as both an allegory of the German occupation of France and a reflection of evil in the world at large.

WORKS TO READ

- *The Outsider* (1942)
- *The Myth of Sisyphus* (philosophical essay, 1942)
- *The Plague* (1947)
- *The Rebel* (non-fiction, 1951)
- *The Fall* (1956)

DID YOU KNOW?

Camus loved to smoke and called his cat Cigarette. He also loved football and played until tuberculosis forced him to quit in 1930. His position was goalkeeper, as it inflicted the least damage on his shoes – his grandmother used to inspect them and she would beat him if she didn't like how worn they looked.

After the war, Camus took an unfashionable stance against Communism and Soviet Russia, embodied in the philosophical work *The Rebel* (1951), which caused a stir among the intellectuals of Paris and cost him the friendship of his former ally Jean-Paul SARTRE.

Camus has been criticized for lacking emotion and sensuality, and certainly his prose tends to be spare and documentary-like. But when he writes of grief and bereavement – when a character in *The Plague* reflects that 'this world without love was like a dead world' – you are right there with him, in the heat and the dust and the despair.

In 1957, at the age of 44, Camus became one of the youngest-ever recipients of the Nobel Prize in Literature. The award oppressed him, as he felt that most of his work was still ahead of him. Little more than two years later he was dead, killed in a road accident in France, leaving the manuscript of an unfinished autobiographical novel, *The First Man*, which he believed would be his masterpiece (and which was eventually published in 1994), to be discovered beside the wrecked car.

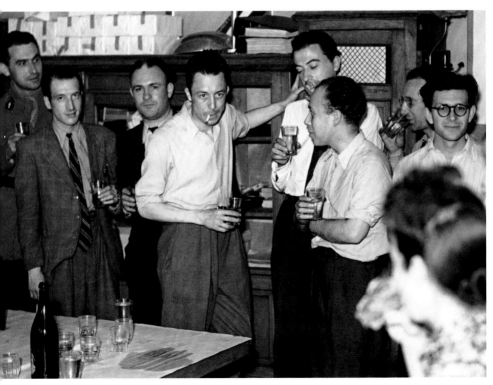

Camus with combat staff in 1944

The Plague, 1947

PETER CAREY

AUSTRALIAN
BORN 1943

'To be an Australian of my age', says this doyen of Australian novelists, 'is to inhabit a colonial situation, where the real place is somewhere else, where your ancestors came from somewhere else.' This sense of displacement is a recurring theme in Carey's novels, even those not set in Australia. The title character of *Jack Maggs* (1997), inspired by the convict Magwitch in Dickens' *Great Expectations* (1861), returns to England after years of penal servitude in Australia, to seek out a boy who was once kind to him. *Parrot and Olivier in America* (2009) has an aristocratic survivor of the French Revolution and his sarcastic English servant exploring the nature of American democracy. In *The Chemistry of Tears* (2012) a 21st-century conservator in a London museum uncovers the story of a Victorian Englishman on a quest to Germany, where as a foreigner he is both derided and swindled. Even the intensely Australian *True History of the Kelly Gang* (2000) begins with Ned Kelly's Irish father being transported to Tasmania.

Other defining features of Carey's work are its complex plots and its frequent changes of viewpoint. From his first published novels, *Bliss* (1981) and the 'ridiculously ambitious' – his words – *Illywhacker* (1985), he has looked at events through the eyes of different characters. In his third, *Oscar and Lucinda* (1988), he goes several steps further, telling his story in 111 very short chapters, which he has likened to a mosaic of tiles that had to be put together to make the whole.

WORKS TO READ

- *Illywhacker* (1985)
- *Oscar and Lucinda* (1988)
- *True History of the Kelly Gang* (2000)
- *Parrot and Olivier in America* (2009)
- *The Chemistry of Tears* (2012)

DID YOU KNOW?

Carey was a Republican and, after winning the Commonwealth Writers Prize for *Jack Maggs*, he was accused of slighting Queen Elizabeth by declining an invitation to meet her. When they did eventually meet, according to Carey the Queen remarked, 'I believe you had a little trouble getting here.'

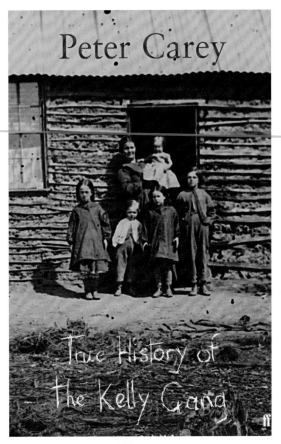

True History of the Kelly Gang, 2000

Oscar and Lucinda was the first of two Carey novels to win the Booker Prize for Fiction (the second was *True History of the Kelly Gang*) and it is probably his best-loved work. Most readers think of it as a doomed love story between two passionate gamblers, one of whom (Lucinda) bets her considerable fortune that the other (Oscar) cannot transport a glass church 400km (250 miles) upriver by barge. But the author's familiar motifs are here, too. Oscar is another displaced person – an English clergyman who goes to Australia to seek a new life – and in the background lurks the theme of Aboriginal culture being destroyed by European immigrants. The love story, Carey says, emerged from other ideas for the book: 'I wasn't thinking about the romantic expectations of the reader.'

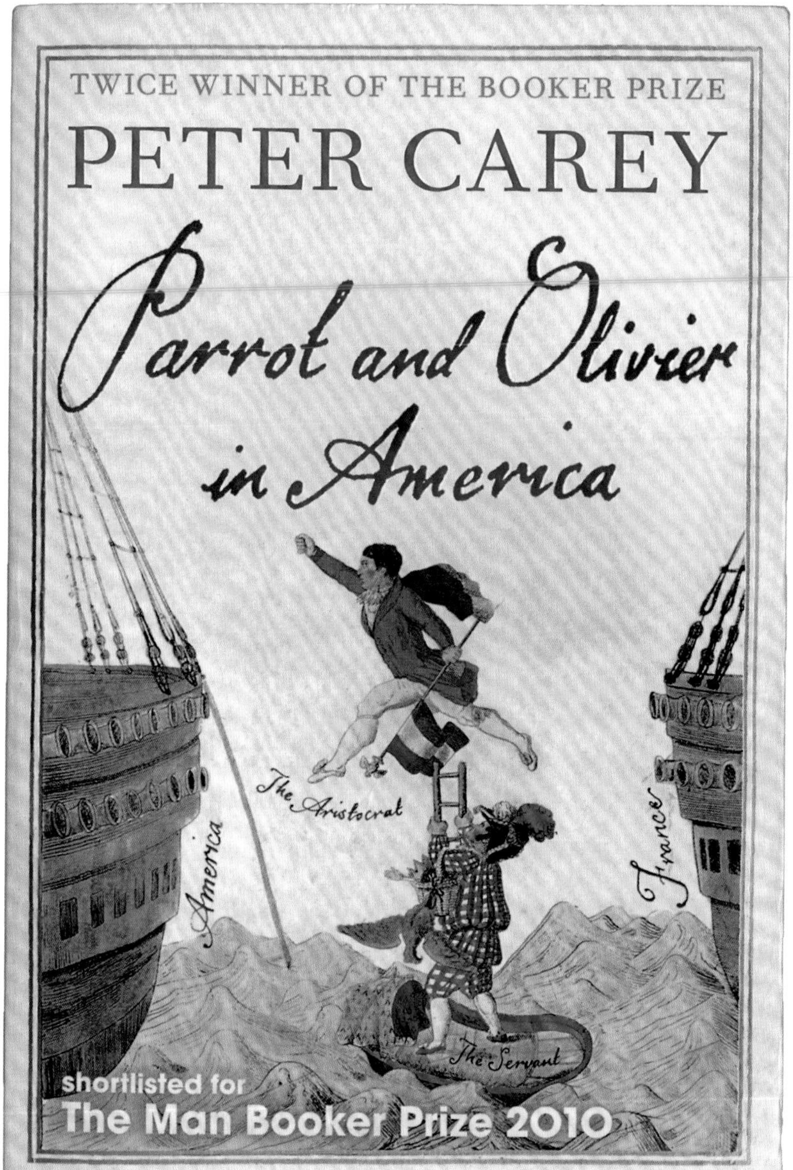

Parrot and Olivier in America, 2009

ANGELA CARTER

BRITISH
1940–92

One word widely applied to the work of Angela Carter is 'virtuoso'; others are 'unique', 'audacious' and 'subversive'. A committed Feminist and Socialist, she saw the novel as having a moral and political function, which she chose to convey in surreal, magical-realist narratives in which her characters stumble from one extraordinary adventure to another – an approach she described as 'a very 18th-century pursuit to make imaginary societies which teach one about our own society'.

Nowhere is this more true than in *The Infernal Desire Machines of Doctor Hoffman* (1972). The civil servant Desiderio (Carter's characters are often aptly named) travels through Nebulous Time in his efforts to find and destroy the Doctor's desire machines: at one point he is adopted by a group of centaurs who are specifically compared to the Houyhnhnms, the talking horses of Jonathan Swift's best-known novel *Gulliver's Travels* (1726).

In similar picaresque style, Sophie Fevvers, the winged circus-performer heroine of Carter's best-known novel *Nights at the Circus* (1984), travels from London to St Petersburg to Siberia, meeting a fortune-telling pig, a regal tiger-tamer and a village shaman along the way. In Carter's last completed work, *Wise Children* (1991), twin chorus girls, Nora and Dora Chance, look back over their lives within an eccentric theatrical family – named, perhaps inevitably, Hazard.

WORKS TO READ
- *The Infernal Desire Machines of Doctor Hoffman* (1972)
- *The Bloody Chamber* (short stories, 1979)
- *Nights at the Circus* (1984)
- *Black Venus*, published in the US as *Saints and Strangers* (short stories, 1985)
- *Wise Children* (1991)

DID YOU KNOW?
Carter's nickname at school was 'tub' and she developed anorexia, 'long before the condition had been properly invented'. Carter believed that, as an acute condition, her anorexia lasted for around two years, but that she still suffered disordered eating until after she gave birth to her son at the age of 42.

Carter writes powerfully, sometimes shockingly, about desire, sex and rape – it is no coincidence that she also wrote a study of women in the work of the Marquis de Sade. Her characters sometimes seem not so much living beings as pawns in her complicated games, but her descriptions, like her imagination, constantly run riot: Doctor Hoffman's first experiments with mirages produce 'pineapples with the colour and texture of strawberries or walnuts which tasted of caramel', while birds 'grew to the size and acquired the temperament of winged jaguars'.

In addition to her novels, Carter was renowned for her exuberant 'revisionings' of folklore and history. The short stories collected in *The Bloody Chamber* (1979) are her take on Bluebeard, Red Riding Hood and others. In the most powerful of the stories in *Black Venus* (1985), 'The Fall River Axe Murders', Lizzie Borden takes an axe and gives her father 40 whacks. It is hot, she has her period (a very Carter touch) and she hates her gluttonous stepmother. The result, Carter makes us feel, is inevitable.

The notion of a universality of human experience is a confidence trick and the notion of a universality of female experience is a clever confidence trick.

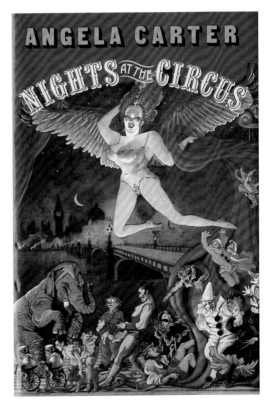

Nights at the Circus, 1984

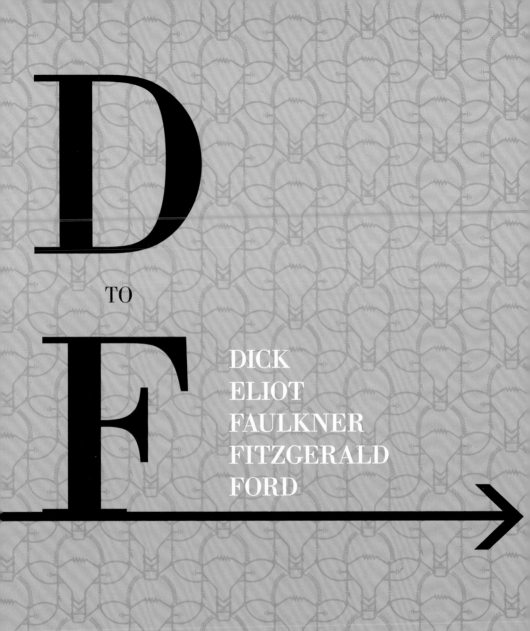

D
TO
F

DICK
ELIOT
FAULKNER
FITZGERALD
FORD

PHILIP K DICK

AMERICAN
1928–82

The 1982 film *Blade Runner*, based on Philip K Dick's novel *Do Androids Dream of Electric Sheep?* (1968), catapulted its author from the sidelines occupied by many science-fiction writers into the mainstream. Unfortunately, Dick was unable to benefit from the film's success: he died the same year, a victim of drug abuse and lifelong mental-health issues.

Dick was born a twin, but his sister died at the age of six weeks: the sense of having lost his 'other self' pervades his work. So, too, does a deep suspicion of technology, which is very much at odds with the optimistic attitude to capitalist life that prevailed in pre-Vietnam America. Watching rural California being 'bulldozed into urban submission' as he grew up, he created in his writing a consumerist and media-obsessed universe in which everything, people included, was trashy and fake. 'If God manifested himself to us,' he wrote, 'he would do so in the form of a product advertised on TV.' Things are rarely what they seem in Dick's work. In *Do Androids Dream of Electric Sheep?* even the lines between humans and androids are blurred: androids resemble humans in almost every way but are incapable of empathy.

Religion and metaphysical questions also feature strongly, as Dick considers what it means to be human. As we might expect, such questions take an unconventional form: in *Ubik* (1969), Ubik is an all-powerful, benevolent – possibly God-like –

WORKS TO READ

- *A Handful of Darkness* (short stories, 1955)
- *Do Androids Dream of Electric Sheep?* (1968)
- *Ubik* (1969)
- *A Scanner Darkly* (1977)
- *VALIS* (1981)

DID YOU KNOW?

Amongst other drugs, copious amounts of amphetamines fuelled Dick's writing. This led to paranoia, but also caught the interest of the FBI. When he returned home one day to find that his house had been trashed, he said, 'Thank God, I'm not crazy…It was a tremendous relief to discover that someone really is after me.'

Still from *A Scanner Darkly* (Richard Linklater), 2006

substance that happens to be available in a spray can. The later novels increasingly reflect their author's experience of drug use: in *A Scanner Darkly* (1977) an undercover narcotics investigator living a double life finds himself investigating himself. In this and other novels of the period Dick managed to portray even schizophrenia in a funny, surreal but sympathetic way.

By the time he wrote *VALIS* – an acronym for Vast Active Living Intelligence System – (1981), Dick had had what he called a 'beatific vision' that restored his awareness of the beauty of the world. He wanted to write a novel in which this vision could be transferred to others. The result is a quest for reality carried out by two aspects of himself, with the division between them never quite clear.

Marginalized for much of his life, Dick is now seen as one of the most significant science-fiction authors. His gloomy views on the impact of technology have a contemporary feel decades after his death.

The basic tool for the manipulation
of reality is the manipulation of words.
If you can control the meaning of words,
you can control the people who must
use them.

99

A Handful of Darkness, 1955

A HANDFUL OF
DARKNESS

PHILIP K.
DICK

RUDLAND

T S ELIOT

ANGLO –
AMERICAN
1888–1965

Born in St Louis, Missouri; educated at Harvard, the Sorbonne and Oxford; director of the publishing house Faber & Faber, where he fostered the careers of, among others, W H Auden, Ted Hughes and Tom Stoppard; distinguished playwright and essayist; posthumously discovered by a whole new audience as the inspiration behind Andrew Lloyd Webber's 1981 musical *Cats*. That's quite a résumé for a man who also wrote some of the most important poetry of the 20th century.

Thomas Stearns Eliot's first major poem, 'The Love Song of J Alfred Prufrock' (1915) – more stream of consciousness than conventional love story – scandalized the literary establishment but is now seen as heralding the birth of modernist poetry, with its unromantic approach to romance.

Then came 'The Waste Land' (1922). Written as five apparently unrelated sections, it draws on the classics, Dante, Shakespeare and the conversation of two young women in a pub; it is a poem about lives that have no meaning in a society that is in a state of collapse; and it captures the despair of the post-World War I generation as no other work of art has done before or since.

Eliot's later works include the playful *Old Possum's Book of Practical Cats* (1939, the inspiration for *Cats*); and the melancholic *Four Quartets* (1936–42), meditations on the passage of time and the importance of silence and sanctuary, based on four places

WORKS TO READ

- 'The Love Song of J Alfred Prufrock' (1915)
- 'The Waste Land' (1922)
- *Murder in the Cathedral* (1935)
- *Old Possum's Book of Practical Cats* (1939)
- *Four Quartets* (1936–42)

DID YOU KNOW?

Eliot was working as a financial analyst for Lloyds bank when 'The Waste Land' made him the most talked-about poet of his age. The business acumen that he acquired at Lloyds was evident when he moved to Faber & Faber: colleague Frank Morley remembered, 'Eliot had a theory you were not likely to lose money on the books you didn't publish.'

Eliot in 1945

that had made a lasting impression on him. They were written after the break-up of his unhappy first marriage and after he had converted to Anglo-Catholicism, a branch of Christianity that – in Eliot's case at least – believed in the power of the conscience and of taking 'the narrow path' to redemption. The difficulties and self-sacrifice his religion advocated are reflected in much of his work.

In addition to poetry, Eliot wrote verse plays – dramas with a theme of redemption, such as *Murder in the Cathedral* (1935), and social-comedies-with-a-message, such as *The Cocktail Party* (1949). He also became one of the great literary critics of his age. His work is not easy – scholars are still debating what 'The Waste Land' means – but it repays the effort. Awarding him the Nobel Prize in Literature in 1948, the committee observed that he 'cut into the consciousness of our generation with the sharpness of a diamond'.

POETRY

T. S. ELIOT
The Waste Land and other Poems

The Waste Land, 1922

WILLIAM FAULKNER

AMERICAN
1897–1962

Often described as the finest of all 20th-century American novelists, the winner of a Nobel Prize and two Pulitzers – one of them posthumous, for *The Reivers* (1962) – William Faulkner set his most successful works in the fictional Mississippi county of Yoknapatawpha, based on his home county of Lafayette and featuring people and places with which he had grown up. There is nothing parochial about his style or his themes, however: he is one of the great chroniclers of the American South.

The Sound and the Fury (1929) is the novel that made his name; it deals with the struggles of the Compson family, Southern aristocrats who have fallen on hard times, and is told from the point of view of three brothers. Parts One and Two, narrated respectively by the simple-minded Benjy and the tormented Quentin, are immensely complicated and non-linear. Faulkner later said that it was the novel on which he had worked longest and hardest, and that to him it was 'the most passionate and moving idea' of any of his novels. It isn't an easy read, though: not until the cynical, money-obsessed Jason takes up the story in Part Three do many readers have a clear idea of what is going on.

Faulkner was extraordinarily productive during the 1930s: the technical complexity of *The Sound and the Fury* is repeated – though never quite equalled – in the acclaimed *As I Lay Dying* (1930), *Light in August* (1932) and *Absalom, Absalom!* (1936).

WORKS TO READ

- *The Sound and the Fury* (1929)
- *As I Lay Dying* (1930)
- *Light in August* (1932)
- *Absalom, Absalom!* (1936)
- *Go Down, Moses* (short story collection, 1942)

DID YOU KNOW?

Faulkner attempted to enlist in the US Army and was rejected for being too short at 5ft 5in (1.65m). Before the medical examination, he reportedly ate and drank lots of bananas and glasses of water in the effort to look heartier. He later managed to join a reservist unit in the British Army.

Still from *The Sound and the Fury* film adaptation (Martin Ritt), 1959

Sanctuary (1931), dealing with rape, murder, prostitution and perjury among the white community in Mississippi, brought financial success and notoriety: *Time* magazine described it as 'outspoken to an almost medical degree'. Faulkner himself, by now with a sizeable family, a 'Southern gentleman' lifestyle and a substantial whiskey habit to support, claimed to have written it for the money. That was certainly his motive for spending time in Hollywood, writing screenplays, which he hated.

66

To understand the world, you must first understand a place like Mississippi.

99

Faulkner was also a master of the short story, notably the seven linked pieces published as *Go Down, Moses* (1942). One of these, 'The Fire and the Hearth', features a black farmer called Lucas Beauchamp, who re-emerges in the novel *Intruder in the Dust* (1948), falsely accused of murder. Faulkner was well aware of the racial tensions in his native state: he based *Intruder in the Dust* on the premise that white people in the South 'owe and must pay a responsibility' to their black neighbours.

Faulkner and his wife outside Rowan Oak, their home near Oxford, Mississippi

F SCOTT
FITZGERALD

AMERICAN

1896–1940

The embodiment of the 'Lost Generation' – young Americans writing about disillusionment in the years following World War I – Francis Scott Key Fitzgerald's life provided him with material for his novels and stories in a way that falls little short of cliché. Born a Catholic in Minnesota, he endured an itinerant childhood that made it difficult for him to make friends; dropped out of Princeton and served briefly in the army; married a socialite, Zelda Sayre, with whom he lived a life marred by, in his case, hard drinking and, in hers, adultery and mental instability, on the French Riviera and subsequently in Paris; had several attempts at screenwriting in Hollywood; became involved with a gossip columnist named Sheilah Graham, who looked rather like the young Zelda; and died of a heart attack at the age of 44. Frankly, you couldn't make it up.

He put it all in his novels. The central character of his first, *This Side of Paradise* (1920), is a youthful drifter, unlucky in love but convinced he has a great literary future; the book earned its author fame and the ability to earn good money from his short stories. *The Beautiful and Damned* (1922) contains thinly veiled portraits of Fitzgerald and Zelda, already troubled by alcohol and uncertain mental health. In *The Great Gatsby* (1925) the enigmatic Jay Gatsby, famous for his lavish parties, is haunted by lost love and a lost past that can never be recaptured; the fact that

WORKS TO READ

- *Tales of the Jazz Age* (short story collection, 1922)
- *The Great Gatsby* (1925)
- *All the Sad Young Men* (short story collection, 1926)
- *Tender is the Night* (1934)
- *The Last Tycoon* (1941)

DID YOU KNOW?

Fitzgerald was named after Francis Scott Key, the lawyer and writer who wrote the poem 'The Star Spangled Banner' during the War of 1812. This poem was later set to music and became the United States' national anthem. The two Francis Scotts were second cousins three times removed.

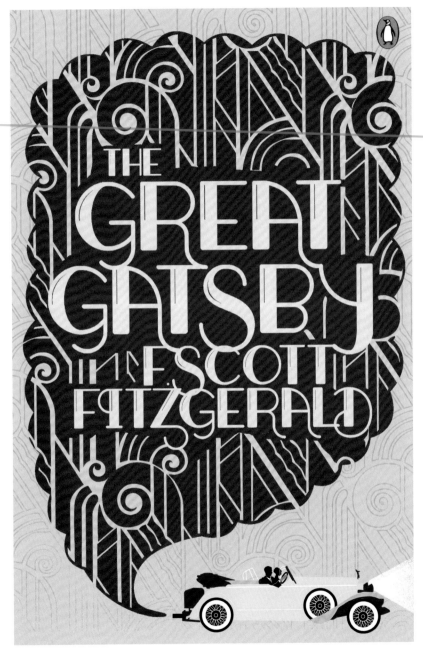

The Great Gatsby, 1925

we see him only through the rather dazzled eyes of his decent, unexciting neighbour Nick adds to his unknowability. *Tender is the Night* (1934) returns to alcoholism and psychiatric disturbance on the Riviera; while in the unfinished *The Last Tycoon* (1941) the Hollywood producer Monroe Stahr becomes obsessed with a young woman who resembles his late wife.

In between novels, Fitzgerald wrote a prodigious number of short stories. From 'The Diamond as Big as the Ritz' (1922), about a family living literally on top of a diamond mountain, to the droll but sorrowful cynicism of the Hollywood hack in *The Pat Hobby Stories* (1940–1), they include many mini-masterpieces – almost all featuring lonely outsiders or optimistic young people who are doomed to disappointment.

Fitzgerald was never happy with what he achieved, yet he has influenced swathes of writers ever since. In Charles Jackson's 1944 novel *The Lost Weekend*, the central character, a lecturer, takes his copy of *The Great Gatsby* from its shelf and says to his literature students, 'There's no such thing as a flawless novel. But if there is, this is it.'

Scott and Zelda, 1920

FORD MADOX FORD

BRITISH

1873–1939

'This is the saddest story I have ever heard,' declares John Dowell, the narrator, in the opening line of Ford Madox Ford's masterpiece *The Good Soldier* (1915). But is it? Can we believe a word this man tells us? Is he truly unaware that the man he idolizes has been having an affair with his wife for the past nine years? Is he, as he suggests throughout the book, too poor a storyteller and too poor a judge of his fellow men to be a fit person to relate their history? Or is he more calculating and altogether more intriguing than that? Who can tell? And that is part of Ford's point. The unreliability of Dowell's narrative mirrors the complex and contradictory truths of the character Edward Ashburnham, the 'good soldier' of the title. He is indeed a good soldier, holder of high military honours. He is also a generous landlord, a considerable philanthropist and a serial womanizer whose affairs provoke more than one unhappy death.

Dowell's narrative is not only unreliable, it is meandering and unchronological, making no concession – until the very end – to the reader's desire to understand what is happening. But as Ford wrote in a memoir about his friend and collaborator Joseph Conrad, 'in your gradual making acquaintance with your fellows you never do go straight forward. You meet an English gentleman at your golf club…You discover, gradually, that he is hopelessly neurasthenic, dishonest in matters of small change, but unexpectedly self-sacrificing, a dreadful liar but a most painfully careful student of

WORKS TO READ

- The *Fifth Queen* trilogy:
  The Fifth Queen: And How She Came to Court (1906);
  Privy Seal (1907); and
  The Fifth Queen Crowned (1908)
- *The Good Soldier* (1915)
- *Joseph Conrad:
  A Personal Remembrance* (1924)
- The *Parade's End* tetralogy:
  Some Do Not... (1924),
  No More Parades (1925),
  A Man Could Stand Up (1926);
  and *Last Post* (1928)

DID YOU KNOW?

Born Ford Madox Hueffer into an his artist family, his grandfather was the artist Ford Madox Brown, who was closely linked to the pre-Raphaelite Brotherhood and whose autobiography Madox Ford wrote. In 1919 Ford dropped Hueffer from his name – partly as he feared it sounded too Germanic and could harm his book sales.

lepidoptera…' These observations inform the way he chooses to tell his story.

The Good Soldier was Ford's twentieth novel; his *Fifth Queen* trilogy (1906–8), about Henry VIII's fifth wife, Katharine Howard, had been his only previous success. After World War I came the *Parade's End* tetralogy (1924–8), which was widely acclaimed for its portrayal not of the horrors of war but of the horrors that war inflicts on its survivors. Its central character, the wealthy, correct and reserved Christopher Tietjens, comes through active service to find himself a dinosaur in a world where everything he believed in is being overturned. As in *The Good Soldier*, society and convention are a veneer, covering the turmoil that lurks just beneath the surface.

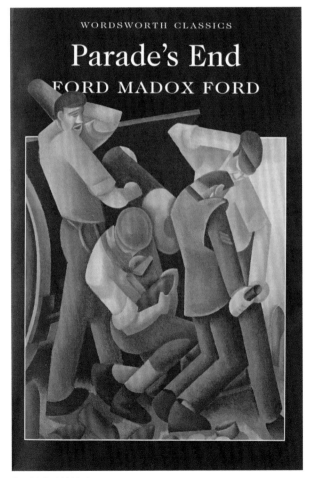

Parade's End, 1924–8

G TO K

GOLDING
GORDIMER
GRASS
GREENE
HEMINGWAY
HESSE
HURSTON
HUXLEY
ISHIGURO
JOYCE
KAFKA

WILLIAM GOLDING

BRITISH
1911–93

Rites of Passage (1980) won William Golding the Booker Prize. At that point he had published nine novels over a period of 26 years and would go on to produce four more. He was awarded the Nobel Prize in Literature in 1983 and knighted five years later. But none of his later achievements could eclipse the fame and extraordinary power of his first novel, *Lord of the Flies* (1954).

The story of a group of schoolboys stranded on an island, it depicts the disintegration of society, as the law and order represented by decent Ralph, wise but irritating Piggy and mystical Simon fail to hold out against the animal instincts of intractable choirboy-turned-hunter Jack. Civilization is symbolized by the conch shell that must be held by anyone wishing to speak at a meeting: when the conch is broken, it is clear that savagery has finally triumphed.

Savagery is never far below the surface in Golding's work: in *The Inheritors* (1955) a band of Neanderthals encounter strange and malevolent creatures who turn out to be humans. *Free Fall* (1959) uses the background of a prisoner-of-war camp to explore how a man can fall apart when social disruption means he has no roots to hold him steady, while in *The Spire* (1964) a man's obsession with building a church tower leads him into the clutches of the devil. In *Rites of Passage*, which is ostensibly about a sea voyage from London to Sydney in the early 19th century, the ritual dunking

WORKS TO READ
- *Lord of the Flies* (1954)
- *Pincher Martin* (1956)
- *Free Fall* (1959)
- *The Spire* (1964)
- *Rites of Passage* (1980) and its sequels *Close Quarters* (1987) and *Fire Down Below* (1989)

DID YOU KNOW?
Golding served in the Royal Navy during World War II and fell in love with the sea. The war, he said, taught him 'that man produces evil as a bee produces honey'. Both the sea and man's capacity for evil feature strongly in his novels.

Golding in 1980

> **"**
>
> Childhood is a disease – a
> sickness that you grow out of.
>
> **"**

of one of the passengers as the ship crosses the equator turns violent and shows how easily the mask of civilization can crack.

The Christian dimension of *The Spire* had already appeared in *Pincher Martin* (1956), when a naval officer washed up on a rock seems to be struggling to survive. In fact, Golding said, he is dead by page two and, because he is a irreligious man who has no concept of God's mercy, he spends the rest of the book creating from his memories a world that gradually disintegrates to become his personal Purgatory.

Golding has been described as the master of the shock ending, encouraging us to reread his books in order to take in what we may have missed first time around. He was writing, he explained, about ideas that concerned him deeply and he wanted others to take them seriously.

ff

WILLIAM GOLDING

Winner of the Nobel Prize for Literature

Lord of the Flies

Lord of the Flies, 1954

NADINE GORDIMER

SOUTH AFRICAN
1923–2014

Born in a mining town just outside Johannesburg, Nadine Gordimer was the great chronicler of life in South Africa during and after apartheid. A long-term member of the African National Congress, she believed that living in South Africa – as she did all her life – involved moral choices. She recorded what she saw, maintaining that it was impossible for any writer dealing with the 'big questions' of life to ignore the political situation. A number of her books were banned in her native country, but she persisted in writing as if censorship did not exist.

Gordimer's first short story was published when she was 15, and she had produced two acclaimed collections before her first novel, *The Lying Days*, appeared in 1953. She went on to write many more and has been ranked alongside Anton Chekhov as a master of the short-fiction genre.

Her novels are all about the troubled relationships between the races. *Occasion for Loving* (1963) chronicles an affair between a wealthy white woman and a black man – not only illicit but also illegal in South Africa at that time. In *The Conservationist* (1974) a white man's hobby farm is disrupted first by the discovery of the body of an unknown black man and later by floods that symbolically threaten the prevailing order. The father of the title character in *Burger's Daughter* (1979) is a white anti-apartheid activist who dies in prison. By the time of *July's People* (1981) the Soweto riots are under way and

WORKS TO READ

- *The Soft Voice of the Serpent* (short stories, 1952)
- *The Conservationist* (1974)
- *Burger's Daughter* (1979)
- *July's People* (1981)
- *Beethoven Was One-Sixteenth Black* (short stories, 2007)

DID YOU KNOW?

Gordimer knew many of South Africa's political activists, including Bram Fischer, Nelson Mandela's defence lawyer. A copy of the banned *Burger's Daughter* was smuggled to Mandela in prison on Robben Island. The letter he wrote to Gordimer after he read it was one of her most treasured possessions.

a liberal white family, frightened for their lives, have to cope with suspicion and hostility when they take refuge in their servant's home village.

The fall of apartheid brings no magical overnight solution. In Gordimer's last novel, *No Time Like the Present* (2012), a mixed-race couple find that 'the fat cats are always with us'. Talking about this book, Gordimer confessed that she and fellow campaigners had been so obsessed with overthrowing the regime that they hadn't given enough thought to what might replace it. Openly critical of the corruption that pervaded everyone from the government official to the traffic cop, she spoke of the partying that had followed the demise of apartheid. The new South Africa, she admitted, was still suffering the effects of 'the morning after'.

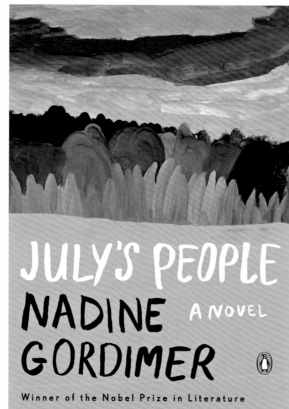

July's People, 1981

> **❝**
>
> The facts are always less than what really happened.
>
> **❞**

Gordimer collecting the W H Smith Literary Award, 1961

GÜNTER GRASS

KASHUBIAN–
GERMAN
1927–2015

Günter Grass was born in the Free City of Danzig; by the end of World War II it had become the Polish port of Gdansk. Thus at the age of 17 he found that everything he'd been brought up to believe in was lost to him, including his birthplace. But loss, he later said, was one of the driving forces of writing: something that has been lost can be reborn if you write about it, and thus you can win it back.

Although he attended art school and remained a keen sculptor all his life, Grass also wrote poetry and met other writers, who encouraged him to attempt a novel. His youth had been so dominated by the 'mistakes and madness' of the Nazi regime, he observed, that when he turned to writing he found his subject matter had been chosen for him. If you want to prevent something like that happening again, he believed, you have to speak out.

Grass's first novel, *The Tin Drum* (1959), remains his most famous. In it, the arrogant and unreliable Oskar Matzerath takes advantage of his diminutive size to become an unseen spectator at many major events that took place under Nazism. Narrating the book from a psychiatric hospital some years later, he summons up his memories by constantly beating on his toy drum. Like Grass himself, Oskar is a subversive character, drawing attention to a history that most Germans of the time would have preferred to forget.

WORKS TO READ

- *The Tin Drum* (1959) and the others of the *Danzig* trilogy: *Cat and Mouse* (1961) and *Dog Years* (1963)
- *The Rat* (1986)
- *Too Far Afield* (1995)
- *Crabwalk* (2002)
- *Peeling the Onion* (2006)

DID YOU KNOW?

Grass was a Hitler 'cub' aged ten and a member of the Hitler Youth at the age of 14. In 1945 he was called to the front and injured, becoming a hospital patient, then a prisoner of war. Grass left the army angry with the German Nationalism that had stolen his childhood and almost destroyed his city.

dtv

Günter Grass

Die Blechtrommel
Roman

Grass's work was always more or less political: *The Rat* (1986) warns against the dangers of environmental destruction and nuclear war; *Too Far Afield* (1995) portrays the recent reunification of Germany as a disaster, particularly for those in the East; and the prose poem 'What Must Be Said' (2012) is overtly critical of Germany's selling arms to Israel. Although all these works sparked controversy, this was nothing compared with the outrage that followed the publication of the 2006 memoir, *Peeling the Onion*, in which Grass revealed that as a teenager he had been conscripted into the Waffen-SS. For many, the news itself and the fact that their left-wing mouthpiece had suppressed it for so long were both shocking betrayals. Rather ruefully defending his decisions towards the end of his life, Grass insisted that in his writing he had always tried to take the view of 'the people' and that 'writers did not have to be on the winners' side'.

Still from *The Tin Drum* film adaptation (Volker Schlöndorff), 1979

The Tin Drum, 1959

GRAHAM GREENE

BRITISH
1904–91

As a boy, Graham Greene attended Berkhamstead School in Hertfordshire, of which his father was headmaster, his family's quarters separated from the rest of the building by a green baize door. Bullied and unhappy, he attempted suicide and underwent psychotherapy. As a young man, he became engaged to a Catholic and took instruction in her faith. Born of these early experiences, the twin themes of separateness and of the fear of Hell and damnation run through his finest books.

In *Brighton Rock* (1938) the doomed teenage mobster Pinkie 'wasn't made for peace, he couldn't believe in it. Heaven was a word; hell was something he could trust.' The persecuted Mexican priest in *The Power and the Glory* (1940) 'carried Hell about with him. Sometimes at night he dreamed of it.' In both *The Heart of the Matter* (1948) and *The End of the Affair* (1951), the torment of the adulterous protagonists (you really can't call Greene's central characters heroes) is increased by their awareness of mortal sin. The contemplation of suicide is never far away and features also in *The Ministry of Fear* (1943), set in London during the Blitz.

Greene travelled widely, partly, he said, to escape the boredom that was his 'besetting sickness'. His works take us with him to the world's remote places: *The Heart of the Matter* is set in Sierra Leone, *A Burnt-Out Case* (1960) in a leper colony in the Congo, *The Quiet American* (1955) in Vietnam and *The Comedians* (1966) in

WORKS TO READ

All of them, all of them. But perhaps:

- *Brighton Rock* (1938)
- *The Heart of the Matter* (1948)
- *The End of the Affair* (1951)
- *Our Man in Havana* (1958)
- *The Comedians* (1966)

DID YOU KNOW?

An established writer who travelled to sensitive areas such as Libya, Cuba and Mexico for his novels, Greene was ripe to be recruited by MI6, as he had the perfect cover. He was recruited by his sister Elizabeth, who also worked there, and his supervisor and friend was Kim Philby, later known in spying circles as the 'Third Man'.

Greene on the set of *Our Man in Havana* (Carol Reed), 1959

Human nature is not black and white but black and grey.

Haiti, under the terrifying regime of 'Papa Doc' Duvalier. In addition to these serious novels, he wrote screenplays – most famously *The Third Man* (1949) – and the more light-hearted works, often thrillers, which he called 'entertainments' – *Stamboul Train* (1932), *Loser Takes All* (1955) and *Our Man in Havana* (1958).

One of Greene's last novels, *Doctor Fischer of Geneva or The Bomb Party* (1980), inspired by the biblical book of Revelation, exposes the overwhelming greed of the rich; *Monsignor Quixote* (1982) is a reflection on Catholicism and Communism, told as a pastiche of the Spanish classic *Don Quixote* (Miguel de Cervantes Saavedra, 1605). Both novels are blackly comic and they bear out Greene's observation that a quotation from poet Robert Browning could have served as an epigraph to all his books: 'Our interest's on the dangerous edge of things. The honest thief, the tender murderer, the superstitious atheist…'

Our Man in Havana, 1958

GRAHAM GREENE
OUR MAN IN HAVANA

ERNEST
HEMINGWAY

AMERICAN
1899–1961

He-man, womanizer, war hero, big-game hunter, drinker, darling of Paris café society: rumours about Ernest Hemingway abounded and he did his best to live up to them. Yet he was a shy man who felt that a writer's work often deteriorated as he grew in public stature.

Wounded in Italy in World War I, Hemingway returned briefly to the US, worked as a journalist, married and, armed with letters of introduction from an older writer friend, moved to Paris. There he became friendly with American writer Gertrude Stein, Irish writer James JOYCE and Spanish artist Pablo Picasso, and was taken under the wing of the American poet Ezra Pound, whose advice to the younger generation was 'make it new'. Determined to become a great writer (and if possible to outshine his friend F Scott FITZGERALD), Hemingway set out to do just that, developing a stripped-down style that was very different from that of American writers of the 19th century. Much imitated, its deceptive simplicity was, at the time, ground-breaking.

A visit to Pamplona, where he fell in love with Spain and bullfighting, inspired Hemingway's first novel, *The Sun Also Rises* (1926), described by a contemporary critic as 'terse, precise and aggressively refreshing prose'. This and *A Farewell to Arms* (1929), drawing on his wartime experiences, established him as one of the great American writers of his generation. The 1930s took him again to Spain, where,

WORKS TO READ

- *The Sun Also Rises* (1926)
- *A Farewell to Arms* (1929)
- *For Whom the Bell Tolls* (1940)
- *The Old Man and the Sea* (1952)
- *The Complete Short Stories of Ernest Hemingway* (The Finca Vigía Edition, 1987)

DID YOU KNOW?

In his final years, Hemingway grew paranoid and believed he was being spied on. At the recommendation of his doctor, he underwent electric shock therapy 15 times. *Spies: The Rise and Fall of the KGB in America*, revealed that Hemingway was indeed on the KGB's list of agents in the US, so he really was followed by the CIA.

THE SUN ALSO RISES

ERNEST HEMINGWAY

like George ORWELL, he came to believe that the Spanish Civil War was a bad war, with wrong on both sides – the attitude that informed *For Whom the Bell Tolls* (1940).

In 1939 he rented a property in Cuba, where he spent most winters for the next 20 years and produced his masterpiece, *The Old Man and the Sea* (1952). For the first time his central character was not a young man setting out to face the world; it was an old, unlucky fisherman struggling to keep afloat – perhaps a portent of Hemingway's own view of the future.

When revolution brought Fidel Castro to power in Cuba in 1959, Hemingway reluctantly succumbed to pressure to leave. He settled in Idaho, but seems never to have been happy there and found it increasingly difficult to write. Finally falling victim to the mental illness that had dogged him for several years, he shot himself at home in July 1961.

Hemingway in Cuba, 1952

There is nothing to writing.
All you do is sit down at
a typewriter and bleed.

The Sun Also Rises, 1926

HERMANN HESSE

GERMAN
1877–1962

One word to sum up Hermann Hesse's novels might be 'alienation'. Brought up in a devout Christian family, Hesse was from an early age resistant to the teachings of the Church and to institutions generally. Yet, he later wrote, he was not without faith: 'I believe in the laws of humanity…and I believe that they will survive the disorder of our time.' His most famous novels, *Siddhartha* (1922), *Steppenwolf* (1927) and *The Glass Bead Game* (1943), are all, in different ways, a search for fulfilment and a warning that enlightenment can come only from within. In *Steppenwolf* in particular, Hesse advises that we have not a single identity, nor even the two (intellectual and animalistic) that the central character believes he has, but many. Happiness comes with an understanding of our multiple selves and an acceptance of the darker aspects of life.

Hesse suffered from depression all his life; after the break-up of his first marriage he moved to the small town of Montagnola in Switzerland and lived there peacefully for more than 40 years. He took up both painting and gardening to help deal with stress and maintained that routine tasks freed the mind to think of other things: he composed most of *The Glass Bead Game* in his head while weeding his garden. It was his last major work and contributed to his winning the Nobel Prize in Literature in 1946. 'The world has decided to stone me to death with prizes, congratulations, telegrams and seven thousand letters,' he wrote, despairingly.

WORKS TO READ

- *Siddhartha* (1922)
- *Steppenwolf* (1927)
- *Narcissus and Goldmund* (1930 – one for the counter-culturalists)
- *The Glass Bead Game* (1949)
- *The Seasons of the Soul: The Poetic Guidance and Spiritual Wisdom of Hermann Hesse* (2011)

DID YOU KNOW?

In 1916 Hesse suffered several crises. The death of his father was followed by his son Martin's serious illness and his wife descended into schizophrenia. Hesse began psychotherapy, which led to him developing an interest in psychoanalysis that influenced him creatively and led to a personal relationship with Carl Jung.

Hesse devoted much of the rest of his life to dealing with his vast correspondence, believing that, as a well-known writer, he had a duty to take a stand on political and spiritual matters. He did not speak to the masses, he said, but only to the individual and his conscience. He continued to write poems, inspired by nature and its parallels with the human experience, until the day he died.

Forty years after its publication, *Steppenwolf*'s disillusionment with the bourgeoisie and its plot device of a 'magical theatre' (with its suggestions of psychedelia) brought the book to the attention of a new young audience – the counter-culture generation of the 1960s. Its rediscovery led to the bestselling author in the German language becoming the most translated European author of the 20th century.

Some of us think holding on makes us strong; but sometimes it is letting go.

Hesse, a keen gardener, in 1956

Penguin Modern Classics

Hermann Hesse
Steppenwolf

Steppenwolf, 1927

ZORA NEALE HURSTON

AMERICAN
1891–1960

The daughter of former slaves, Zora Neale Hurston grew up in the oldest black municipality in the US, Eatonville, Florida. 'When you grow up in a town where everyone looks like you, you don't think about colour,' she wrote later. As a teenager she left home to escape a stepmother she detested, took odd jobs to support herself and, at the age of 26, lied about her age in order to qualify for free high school education in Baltimore. (The lie endured: her gravestone records that she was ten years younger than she actually was.) The success of her first published story introduced her to literary circles and earned her the sponsorship of author Annie Nathan Meyer. In 1928 – aged 37 – Hurston became the first black person to graduate from Barnard, the prestigious New York women's college affiliated to Columbia University.

By this time the Harlem Renaissance – 'the African-American Age of Enlightenment' – was in full swing: the success of jazz, blues and the writings of black authors, among whom Hurston soon became prominent, was raising questions of identity for black Americans as never before. Having studied anthropology, she was eager to advance the wider public's knowledge of her race's culture, and she set about researching and preserving its folklore: the result was an acclaimed collection of stories, *Mules and Men* (1935). She had already published a novel, *Jonah's Gourd Vine* (1934) and soon followed this with her masterpiece, *Their Eyes Were Watching God* (1937).

WORKS TO READ

- *Color Struck* (play, 1925)
- *Jonah's Gourd Vine* (1934)
- *Mules and Men* (folktales, 1935)
- *Their Eyes Were Watching God* (1937)
- *Dust Tracks on a Road* (autobiography, 1942)

DID YOU KNOW?

Hurston's father was elected Mayor of her home town of Eatonville and he went on to be the preacher at the town's largest church. Hurston frequently used Eatonville as a backdrop for her stories, including much of *Their Eyes were Watching God*.

Written largely in the African-American vernacular she had heard as a child, it is set in Florida and is the story of Janie, a mixed-race girl forced into a loveless marriage. She runs away with an ambitious man who is so concerned with social position that he stifles her emotionally; and she finally finds fulfilment with someone who wants her by his side rather than on a pedestal. Because of its language, many black critics felt that the book was disparaging to African-Americans, though its only overt racism comes from a light-skinned black woman who despises the darker members of her own community.

Despite a successful autobiography, *Dust Tracks on a Road* (1942), Hurston died in poverty and obscurity. It was only after the novelist and poet Alice Walker rediscovered her in the 1970s that she became acknowledged as one of the foremost of African-American authors.

Hurston playing the mama drum in 1937

Sometimes, I feel discriminated against, but it does not make me angry. It merely astonishes me. How can any deny themselves the pleasure of my company? It's beyond me.

Jonah's Gourd Vine, 1934

"A bold and beautiful book, many a
page priceless and unforgettable."
CARL SANDBURG

Zora Neale Hurston

AUTHOR OF *Their Eyes Were Watching God*

JONAH'S GOURD VINE

WITH A FOREWORD BY
RITA DOVE
AND AN AFTERWORD BY
HENRY LOUIS GATES, JR.

A Novel

HARPER**PERENNIAL** MODERN**CLASSICS**

P.S.
INSIGHTS,
INTERVIEWS
& MORE...

ALDOUS
HUXLEY

BRITISH
1894–1963

Aldous Huxley was born into a distinguished scientific and literary family: his grandfather, T H Huxley, had been a renowned supporter of the naturalist Charles Darwin; on his mother's side he was related to the poet Matthew Arnold. As a young man he spent time at Garsington Manor, home of the noted patron of the arts Lady Ottoline Morrell; through her he met Virginia WOOLF, D H LAWRENCE, T S ELIOT, the philosopher Bertrand Russell and other intellectuals of the day. He also developed an interest in pacifism, which would colour his world view for the rest of his life.

His first published novel, *Crome Yellow* (1921), although full of entertaining caricatures of the Garsington circle, reflected the fear of the future that Huxley's generation felt as pre-World War I values crumbled. In the more ambitious and complex *Point Counter Point* (1928), he began to explore the negative effects the modern technological world had on human principles and behaviour.

These ideas are further developed in Huxley's best-known work, *Brave New World* (1932). In it, he portrays a dictatorship under which babies are mass-produced in a laboratory and divided into castes, designated from alpha to epsilon, with the lower ranks chemically treated to stunt their growth and intelligence so that they are suited to menial tasks. The use of mind-controlling drugs and propaganda means that no one is unhappy – a prospect that greatly alarmed Huxley. One of his worst fears, he

WORKS TO READ

- *Crome Yellow* (1921)
- *Point Counter Point* (1928)
- *Brave New World* (1932)
- *Eyeless in Gaza* (1936)
- *Brave New World Revisited* (essays, originally published as *Enemies of Freedom*, 1958)

DID YOU KNOW?

Huxley and the creator of Narnia, C S Lewis, both died on 22 November 1963, the same day as US President John F Kennedy. Lewis died shortly after the President was shot, with Huxley being the last of the three men to pass away. He was remembered with a funeral in Los Angeles and a walk at Mulholland Drive.

Brave New World, 1932

said later in life, was a society in which slaves did not have to be coerced because they loved their servitude.

Along with an increasing advocacy of pacifism came an interest in mysticism and the changes in the body that could be brought about by meditation, fasting and drugs: the cynical protagonist of *Eyeless in Gaza* (1936) eventually finds enlightenment through mysticism. Huxley himself experimented with psychedelic drugs under the auspices of the psychiatrist Humphrey Osmond and wrote a book about his 'tripping' experience, *The Doors of Perception* (1954).

Huxley's views and fears were remarkably prescient. Interviewed in 1958, he spoke of the dangers of overpopulation; his concern that technology could be used for ill as well as for good; the way politicians were 'merchandized' as if they were soap or toothpaste; and the pharmaceutical revolution that made a dictatorship controlling the minds of its people a real possibility. The brave new world he had foretold a quarter of a century earlier was, perhaps, just around the corner.

Huxley in 1926

If most of us remain ignorant of ourselves, it is because self-knowledge is painful and we prefer the pleasures of illusion.

KAZUO ISHIGURO

JAPANESE-
BRITISH
BORN 1954

One recurrent theme of Kazuo Ishiguro's novels is loss: Etsuko in *A Pale View of Hills* (1982) struggling to come to terms with her daughter's suicide; the unexpressed love between butler and housekeeper in a stately home in *The Remains of the Day* (1989); the quest for their missing son that makes the elderly Axl and Beatrice leave their home in *The Buried Giant* (2015). Alongside this is the acceptance of unacceptable situations – never more so than in *Never Let Me Go* (2005), the central characters of which seem unperturbed to discover that they are clones who exist only to act as organ donors. Ishiguro has said that he is interested in the passive way in which many of us accept the unsatisfactory relationships and unfulfilling jobs that seem to be our lot in life, and admits that some of his characters are 'almost infuriatingly accepting' of their positions. As readers, we combine admiration of their stoicism with a strong desire for them just to get a grip.

Although Ishiguro's novels have won many awards, his use of language divides critics. It's not that he is experimental in a Joycean way; rather that he creates a form of English to suit the individual work, with the result that it sometimes reads like a translation. To a reader unfamiliar with Japanese, *An Artist of the Floating World* (1986) seems full of lilting Japanese cadences; the Kafkaesque *The Unconsoled* (1995) could have been translated from Czech; and in *The Buried Giant*, set in a post-Arthurian

WORKS TO READ

- *An Artist of the Floating World* (1986)
- *The Remains of the Day* (1989)
- *The Unconsoled* (1995)
- *Never Let Me Go* (2005)
- *Nocturnes: Five Stories of Music and Nightfall* (short stories, 2009)

DID YOU KNOW?

Born in Nagasaki just nine years after it was hit by the nuclear bomb, Ishiguro left Japan with his family aged five and didn't return until almost 30 years later – as a participant in the Japan Foundation Short-Term Visitors Program. He eventually became a British citizen in 1982.

Still from *The Remains of the Day* film adaptation (James Ivory), 1993

Britain, the characters speak to each other in a stilted language obviously intended to represent some early version of English. For some, this comes across as banal. For others, the slightly awkward language of *The Unconsoled* reflects the unease of the central character, Ryder, a concert pianist socially out of his depth in his tour of Eastern Europe, while the simple speech in *The Buried Giant* reflects Axl's and Beatrice's trusting natures. Bear in mind that Ishiguro was born in Japan and came to the UK at the age of five, and that he is also a songwriter with a musician's ear for tone and rhythm. Then read his books and decide for yourself.

Winner of the Whitbread Book of the Year
Shortlisted for the Booker Prize

Kazuo Ishiguro

An Artist of the Floating World

'An exquisite novel.' *Observer*

By the author of *The Remains of the Day*
and *Never Let Me Go*

ff

An Artist of the Floating World, 1986

JAMES JOYCE

IRISH

1882–1941

We celebrate the birthday of Scottish poet Robert Burns and, to a lesser extent, acknowledge Shakespeare's, but Leopold Bloom, the Jewish hero of James Joyce's masterwork *Ulysses* (1922), is surely the only character from fiction to have a day devoted to him. Every year on 16 June – the day on which the action of *Ulysses* takes place – Dubliners (and Joyce enthusiasts the world over) take to the streets and pubs to revel in Bloomsday.

On the face of it, *Ulysses*, inspired by Homer's *Odyssey*, recounts Bloom's wanderings, and those of the young intellectual Stephen Dedalus, through Dublin on that day in 1904. On a deeper level, it is a study of a modern Everyman portrayed in epic terms, experiencing a series of what Joyce called 'epiphanies' – finding spectacular truths in ordinary things. It is also a huge experiment with form and language, with interior monologues and stream of consciousness. In many people's assessment, it is the greatest novel of the 20th century.

Joyce left his native Ireland with his future wife, Nora Barnacle, in 1904 and lived the rest of his life in Europe. But as he moved from Italy to Switzerland to France and finally back to Switzerland, Dublin remained at the centre of his writing. So accurate is the portrayal of the city in *Ulysses* that, Joyce claimed, if Dublin were to be destroyed it could be reconstructed from his novel.

WORKS TO READ
- *Dubliners* (short stories, 1914)
- *A Portrait of the Artist as a Young Man* (1916)
- *Ulysses* (1922)
- *Finnegans Wake* (if you dare, 1939)
- *James Joyce* by Richard Ellmann (one of the greatest biographies ever written, 1959)

DID YOU KNOW?
Ulysses takes place on t16 June, the date of Joyce's first date with his future wife, Nora Barnacle, in 1904. They had a passionate love affair and wrote each other many erotic letters, one of which sold for a record £240,000 (about $350,000) at Sotheby's in 2004.

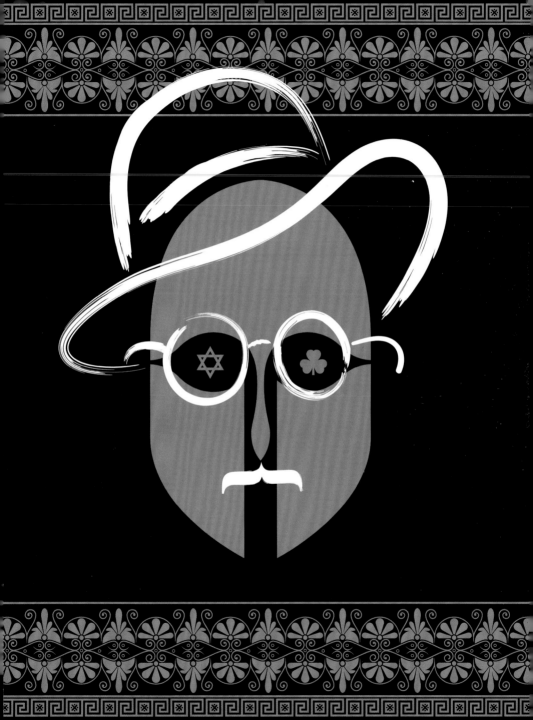

JAMES JOYCE

Dubliners

Dubliners, 1914

There is not past, no future; everything flows in an eternal present.

His first published book, *Dubliners* (1914), was a collection of short stories the themes of which – the pernicious influence of the Church, unhappy marriages, the sorrow of wasted lives – recur throughout his work. It was followed by *A Portrait of the Artist as a Young Man* (1916), the partly autobiographical novel in which Stephen Dedalus (whose obsession with his writing technique is a satirical reflection on Joyce's own youth) makes his first appearance. *Ulysses* was published in a limited edition in Paris in 1922, but its explicit sexual references led to it being banned in the UK and US until the mid-1930s.

Finally, in 1939, came *Finnegans Wake*, the experimental language of which had taken the author 17 years to perfect and makes it far from easy to read – though it is said to be exhilarating to hear when read aloud in an Irish accent. One critic has called it 'a form of high falutin, Gaelic, literary rap. Ireland talking in her sleep.' Joyce himself, when asked what the novel was about, replied, 'I've put in so many enigmas and puzzles that it will keep the professors arguing for centuries over what I meant. And that's the only way of assuring one's immortality.'

Joyce with his publisher, Sylvia Beach, Paris, 1922

FRANZ KAFKA

CZECH

1883–1924

Of all the writers in this book, Franz Kafka is the one whose name has the strongest resonance. Even if we haven't read his work, we know that 'Kafkaesque' means nightmarish, threatening, full of unanswered questions. Why does travelling salesman Gregor Samsa wake up one morning to find he has been transformed into a giant insect (in *Metamorphosis*, 1915)? Why has harmless bank cashier Josef K been arrested and why does his own lawyer think his case is hopeless (*The Trial*, written in 1914–15, published in 1925)? Why can the character known only as K not gain access to the authorities governing the village in which he wishes to live (*The Castle*, written about 1922, published 1926)? We don't know, we will never find out and it is deeply troubling. Kafka's protagonists are often battling against impenetrable bureaucracy, but that is not all: they are alienated from society, and suffering inexplicably from guilt and the unfocused fear the existentialists call angst.

This fear of an all-pervading, arbitrary power begins to make sense when you consider the author's relationship with his father. In a 45-page letter written when Franz was 36, in an attempt to explain to Kafka senior why he was still afraid of him, he recalled an incident when, as a child, he had called out for a glass of water in the night. The furious father had lifted the boy out of bed and put him out on the balcony to freeze until morning. 'I was quite obedient after that period,' Franz wrote, with chilling

WORKS TO READ

- *Metamorphosis* (1915)
- *The Trial* (1925)
- *The Castle* (1926)
- *Dearest Father. Stories and Other Writings* (1954)
- *The Diaries of Franz Kafka, 1910–23* (1988)

DID YOU KNOW?

Kafka was the eldest of six children, born into a German-Jewish family in Prague. His two younger brothers both died in childhood. Kafka himself succumbed to tuberculosis 15 years before the outbreak of World War II, and his three younger sisters all perished in Nazi concentration camps.

understatement, 'but it did me so much incalculable inner harm.' Typically, Franz's timorous mother thought it would be better if her husband didn't read the letter and gave it back to her son. (It was published in *Dearest Father. Stories and Other Writings*, 1954, when all involved were safely dead.)

Unsurprisingly, Kafka grew up with an overwhelming sense of self-loathing, which manifested itself in repeated failed relationships with women and in the fact that most of his work was left unfinished, because he could never be satisfied with anything he had done.

As a final act of self-disgust, when he was dying of tuberculosis, he instructed his friend Max Brod to destroy all his papers. Posterity has reason to be grateful to Brod for ignoring this request and for publishing not only Kafka's novels and stories but his soul-baring diaries and letters, too.

Every revolution evaporates and leaves behind only the slime of a new bureaucracy.

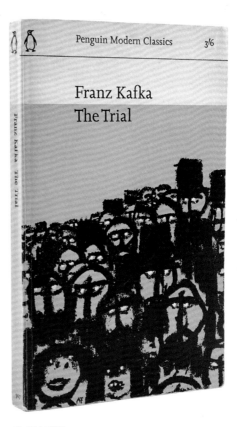

The Trial, 1925

L to N

LAWRENCE
LESSING
LISPECTOR
LORCA
MAHFOUZ
MANN
MÁRQUEZ
MISHIMA
MORRISON
MURDOCH
NABAKOV
NARAYAN

D H LAWRENCE

BRITISH
1885–1930

There's no denying that he has a certain reputation. Yes, *Lady Chatterley's Lover* (1928) was banned, as were some of his earlier novels, and, yes, two men wrestled naked in front of the fire in *Women in Love* (1920), but there is much more to Lawrence than nudity and four-letter words. It has been said that no one wrote more understandingly about desire. He makes us sympathize deeply with the errant Constance Chatterley: the description of her marital home, on the edge of a mining village with 'rows of wretched, small, begrimed, brick houses, with black slate roofs for lids, sharp angles and wilful, blank dreariness', shows us that Connie – used to Kensington and the countryside and married to a paralysed husband – is screaming with boredom and frustration before she even sets eyes on the gamekeeper.

David Herbert Lawrence was born in just such a Midlands mining community and set his first success, *Sons and Lovers* (1913), there. Largely autobiographical, it explores a young artist's sexual awakening, but also his intense relationship with his mother. Lawrence had already caused uproar by eloping with a married woman, Frieda Weekley (née von Richthofen), whom he married in 1914. He added to his scandalous reputation with *The Rainbow* (1915), a precursor to *Women in Love*, with its free and frank exploration of sexual desire, both heterosexual and – outrageously for the time – between women.

WORKS TO READ
- *The Rainbow* (1915)
- *Women in Love* (1920)
- *Birds, Beasts and Flowers* (poetry, 1923)
- *Lady Chatterley's Lover* (1928)
- *Collected Short Stories* (2014)

DID YOU KNOW?
Lawrence's open opposition to militarism, coupled with his wife Frieda's German parentage, meant that during World War I they were treated with suspicion. In 1917, after continuous harassment, the Lawrences were ousted from their home in Cornwall with just three days' notice under the Defence of the Realm Act.

Lady Chatterley's Lover caused a scandal upon its British publication in 1960

Be a good animal, true to your animal instincts.

Lawrence, who was openly critical of Britain's role in World War I, was accused of spying; Frieda's German descent also attracted the attention of the authorities. In 1919, to escape persecution and poverty, the couple left England and went on what he called a 'savage pilgrimage', travelling widely through Europe and as far afield as Mexico and Australia. They never lived in England again: despite its gritty mining-country setting, *Lady Chatterley's Lover* was written in Italy. Having contracted tuberculosis, Lawrence died in France at the age of only 44.

The passage of time has re-established Lawrence's reputation not as a purveyor of porn but as an imaginative portrayer of the joys of sex and sexual freedom. His short stories and poems, as well as his novels, are alive with the wonders of nature, the horrors of industrialization and what Frieda called 'the splendour of living, the hope of more and more life…a heroic and immeasurable gift'.

PENGUIN BOOKS

LADY CHATTERLEY'S LOVER

D.H. LAWRENCE

COMPLETE AND **3/6** UNEXPURGATED

Lady Chatterley's Lover, 1928. Pictured is the notorious Penguin edition of 1960.

DORIS LESSING

BRITISH
1919–2013

In her life, as in her writing, Doris Lessing pushed the boundaries, refusing to let herself stand still. As a child in what was then Southern Rhodesia (now Zimbabwe), she escaped the repression of white society to explore the African bush. Moving to England as a young woman, she felt alienated by both the intellectual scene and the greyness of post-war London; although she espoused many causes, she remained an outsider and an observer for the rest of her life. She was an active member of the Communist Party, but later became disillusioned and turned her attention to Sufism, the mystical dimension of Islam. And while distancing herself from the Feminist movement, in *The Golden Notebook* (1962) she wrote one of the iconic 'feminist novels' of the 20th century.

Lessing's literary output ranges from short stories to autobiography, from poetry to opera libretti. Her novels reflect her African childhood, her experience of mental illness, social and political struggle, and her concerns with the future of the planet – a bleak one, if *Mara and Dann* (1999) is to be believed. Whatever her subject matter, she delves with unflinching honesty into the essence of human relationships, sparing neither the reader nor herself.

She caused controversy from the beginning with *The Grass is Singing* (1950), which deals with the tensions between races in southern Africa, and even more so with *The*

WORKS TO READ

- *The Grass is Singing* (1950)
- *The Golden Notebook* (1962)
- *Briefing for a Descent Into Hell* (1971)
- *African Laughter: Four Visits to Zimbabwe* (memoir, 1992)
- *Under My Skin* and *Walking in the Shade* (volumes 1 and 2 of her autobiography, 1994 and 1997)

DID YOU KNOW?

Lessing received the Nobel Prize in 2007. At 88, she was the oldest person to receive the Literature prize, and the third oldest recipient across all categories. She was also only the eleventh woman to receive the Nobel Prize in Literature in the awards', at the time, 106-year history.

Golden Notebook, which examines women's lives, the way they speak to each other and, most daringly, their attitudes to sex in a way that had never been done before. Writing it, Lessing said, changed her own way of thinking and crystallized her distrust of enforced divisions on the grounds of gender, colour, class and ideology. One of her main themes was fragmentation, both of the individual and of society, but she also explored the connections that brought people closer together. Particularly in what she called her 'space fiction' (the *Canopus in Argos: Archives* series, 1979–83) and 'inner-space fiction' (*Briefing for a Descent into Hell*, 1971), she emphasized the insignificance of humankind, but persisted in seeking a meaning in life.

She continued to publish until she was almost 90, and at 88 became the oldest-ever recipient of the Nobel Prize in Literature. 'I've won all the prizes in Europe, every bloody one,' she said, 'so I'm delighted to win them all. It's a royal flush.'

Think wrongly, if you please, but in all cases think for yourself.

Lessing demonstrating in Trafalgar Square with John Osborne, 1961

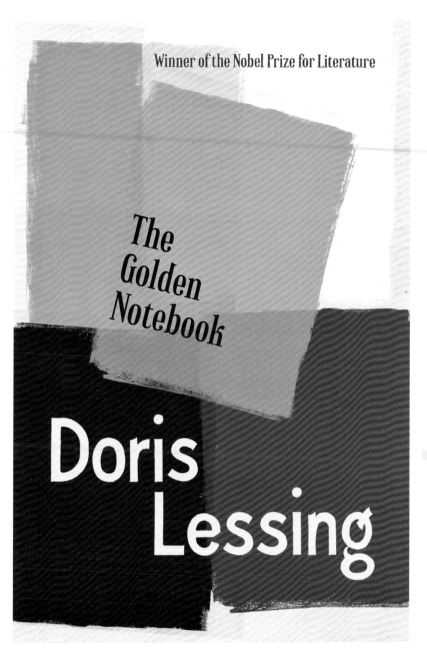

The Golden Notebook, 1962

CLARICE LISPECTOR

BRAZILIAN
1920–77

It has been said that she looked like Marlene Dietrich, wrote like Virginia WOOLF and was the most important Jewish writer since Franz KAFKA; her name has been linked to those of Katherine Mansfield, Albert CAMUS and Anton Chekhov. Hailed in Brazil as having 'shifted the centre of gravity around which the Brazilian novel had been revolving for about 20 years', she is surprisingly little known elsewhere.

Taken to Brazil as a baby by her Jewish parents, Clarice Lispector married a diplomat and travelled with him to Europe and the US, but returned home when her marriage broke up in 1959. 'I am a Brazilian,' she wrote, 'and that is that.' However, as a refugee, albeit a very glamorous one, she never quite fitted in, and her writing reflects a sense of isolation and alienation. She often wrote in interior monologue, concentrating on getting inside someone's head in a given moment, rather than on plot or character development.

Her first novel, *Near to the Wild Heart* (1943), published when she was only 23, caused a sensation in Brazil and made her a national celebrity. She produced eight more, the two most famous of which have been described as more like meditations on time and language than conventional fiction. *The Passion According to G H* (1964) concerns a woman who, cleaning out the room of a departed maid, accidentally squashes a cockroach in the wardrobe door. So fascinated is she by the dying insect

WORKS TO READ
- *Near to the Wild Heart* (1943)
- *The Passion According to G H* (1964)
- *The Stream of Life* (1973)
- *Family Ties* (short stories, 1960)
- *The Complete Stories* (2015)

DID YOU KNOW?
With her father's encouragement, Lispector studied law at the elite National Law Faculty of the University of Brazil and briefly contemplated becoming a prison lawyer rather than a writer. At the law school, there were no other Jews and only three women.

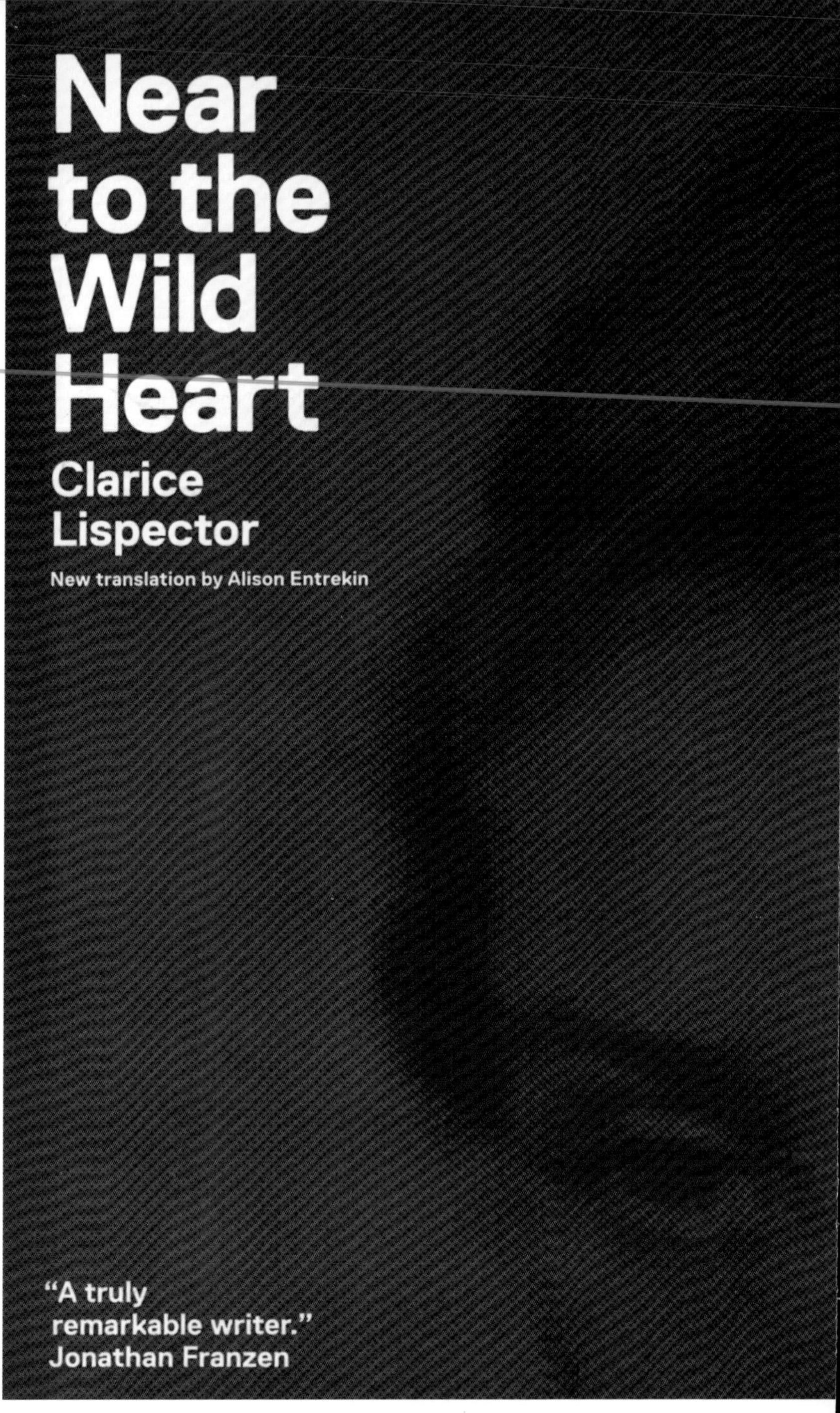

Near to the Wild Heart

Clarice Lispector

New translation by Alison Entrekin

"A truly
remarkable writer."
Jonathan Franzen

Near to the Wild Heart, 1943

that her obesesion keeps her trapped in the room with it, resulting in a stomach-churning conclusion. In the acclaimed *The Stream of Life* (1973) an artist becomes obsessed with trying to isolate individual moments in time.

Lispector was also a master of the short story, the best of which are collected in *Family Ties* (1960). Although she shows the occasional touch of sardonic humour, she is more concerned with humiliation, disorientation, resentment and fear. In 'Happy Birthday', an elderly grandmother spits violently on the floor in disgust at the family gathered to celebrate her birthday; in 'The Buffalo' a woman visits the zoo, hoping to find an animal that will teach her how to hate; in 'The Imitation of the Rose', a woman recovering from a nervous breakdown gives away a bunch of roses because their beauty disturbs her. There are few happy endings with Lispector, and she forcefully gives the lie to those who maintain that women writers cannot cope with abstract and wide-ranging ideas.

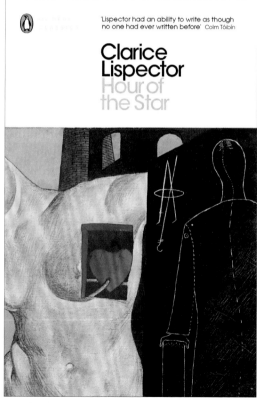

Hour of the Star, 1977

Everything I do not know forms the greater part of me: This is my largesse.

FEDERICO GARCÍA LORCA

SPANISH
1898–1936

On the face of it, Federico García Lorca had everything going for him. He was a talented artist and musician as well as a poet. He was lively, witty and charismatic. As a student in Madrid he became friends with the great creative figures of the day, notably the artist Salvador Dalí and the film director Luis Buñuel. He soon achieved success and fame to complement the wealth he had been born with.

Yet as a homosexual, left-winger and defender of the repressed and the marginalized in deeply conservative southern Spain, Lorca made powerful enemies. When civil war broke out in 1936, his home city of Granada quickly fell to the Fascists; supporters of the Republican government were murdered by the thousands. Lorca is believed to have been executed by Fascist firing squad and buried in a communal grave with others who had suffered the same fate.

One of his supposed sins was attacking traditional Catholic values. Particularly in plays such as *Blood Wedding* (1932), *Yerma* (1934) and *The House of Bernarda Alba* (1936), he created strong, passionate female characters and supported their right to love and marry whomever they chose. Yet these heroines all end tragically, driven to desperate acts by a society that keeps them 'in their proper place'. Obsession, vengeance, honour, dishonour and fate are recurring themes.

Lorca's work is deeply rooted in Andalusian folklore, in which flowers and trees have

WORKS TO READ

- *Gypsy Ballads* (poetry, 1928)
- *Blood Wedding* (play, 1932)
- *Yerma* (play, 1934)
- *The House of Bernarda Alba* (play, 1936)
- *Poet in New York* (poetry, 1940)

DID YOU KNOW?

The set and costumes for Lorca's play *Mariana Pineda* (1923–5), first performed in Barcelona in 1927, were designed by Salvador Dalí. The friendship between Lorca and Dalí lasted from 1923 to 1936, up until Lorca's execution. On Dalí's own deathbed, five decades later, one of his nurses said that of all he said, she could only understand 'my friend Lorca'.

symbolic meaning, and blood is an emblem of both life and death. It also displays classical influences, with minor characters serving as commentators in the manner of a Greek tragedy. Often these personages have no individuality, being described merely as Mother, Father, Bride or Neighbour. Even the title character of *Yerma*, a woman trapped in a passionless marriage and desperate to have children, has no real name of her own: the word simply means 'barren'.

Lorca's best-known collection of poetry, *Gypsy Ballads* (1928), reflects his interest in another marginalized group, while *Poet in New York* (published posthumously in 1940) shows his horror at capitalism American-style, at the treatment of blacks and at the human tragedy induced by the Wall Street Crash of 1929.

His style increasingly experimental, his imagery rich and vivid, his themes daring and uninhibited, Lorca's early death leaves us regretting the works he did not live to write.

"

There is nothing more poetic and terrible than the battle of the skyscrapers with the heavens that cover them.

"

Poet in New York, 1940

Gypsy Ballads, 1928

FEDERICO GARCIA LORCA

ROMANCERO GITANO

SÉPTIMA EDICIÓN

ESPASA-CALPE, S. A.

NAGUIB MAHFOUZ

EGYPTIAN
1911–2006

A committed Egyptian Nationalist, supporter of freedom of speech and critic of Islamic extremism, Naguib Mahfouz observed, 'In all my writings, you will find politics. You may find a story which ignores love or any other subject, but not politics; it is the very axis of our thinking.' Even the part-autobiographical *Mirrors* (1972), a series of vignettes of people who had passed through the life of the unnamed writer-narrator, can be read as a political history of modern Egypt. He lived in Cairo all his long life and from there brought Arab literature to the attention of the world.

Among his 34 novels, 350 short stories, film scripts and plays, his most famous work is the trio of novels known as the *Cairo* trilogy (1956–7). This concerns three generations of the al-Jawad family coming to terms with changes in their homeland, from the 1919 revolt against British occupation, through the early years of independence and into World War II, when Egypt had to deal with both the threat of invasion and internal turmoil between the powerful Muslim Brotherhood, left-wing activists and royalists.

These conflicts are represented in the efforts of the various members of the al-Jawad family to find meaning in their lives. The patriarch, al-Sayyid Ahmad, insists on strict religious observance and family honour while drinking and philandering outside the home; his son Fahmy is martyred in the Nationalist cause; and, as the years go

WORKS TO READ

- *Midaq Alley* (1947)
- The *Cairo* trilogy: *Palace Walk* (1956), *Palace of Desire* (1957) and *Sugar Street* (1957)
- *Mirrors* (1972)
- *Stories from our Neighbourhood* (autobiographical short stories, 1975)
- *The Day the Leader was Killed* (1983)

DID YOU KNOW?

Awarded the Nobel Prize in Literature in 1988, Mahfouz remains the only Arab to have received this accolade. Known for his dislike of leaving Egypt, he sent his two daughters, Fatima and Umm Kulthum, to collect the award on his behalf. Egyptian President Hosni Mubarak described Mahfouz as 'a cultural light who brought Arab literature to the world'.

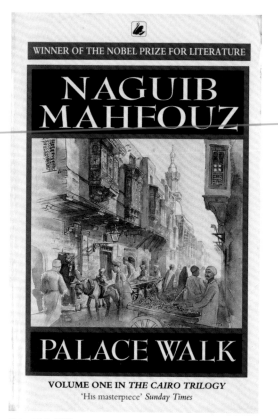

Palace Walk, 1956

by, one grandson espouses Communism, a second religious fundamentalism and the third succumbs to the lure of political advancement through 'influence'. In the meantime, Fahmy's younger brother Kamal remains an intellectual philosopher, unable to commit to any cause and unwilling to marry out of fear of commitment and the loss of liberty this will bring. Throughout the novels characters ask themselves, 'Is this the answer?' 'Will this make me happy?' 'Will this make me a better person?' and the reader, with the author, thinks, 'Who knows? Probably not.' In the background, most of the women remain quietly at home, caring for husbands and children or waiting to be married off, some contentedly, some not.

Mahfouz's novels teem with life, humour and compassion – his Cairo has been likened to Charles Dickens's London. He raises questions about life, family, love, religion and politics that remain as relevant today as when he asked them half a century ago. And there are no glib answers.

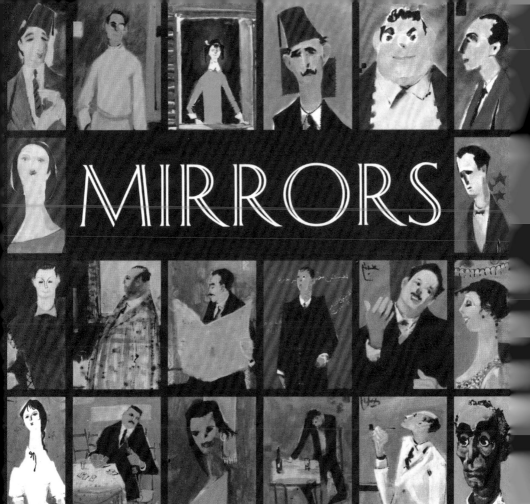

MIRRORS

NAGUIB MAHFOUZ

ILLUSTRATED BY
SEIF WANLI

THOMAS MANN

GERMAN

1875–1955

In the early years of the 20th century, the distinguished author Gustav von Aschenbach, ageing and lonely, breaks away from his domestic routine and travels to Venice, hoping that a visit to the city will replenish his spirit and enable him to write again. Staying at his elegant hotel is a Polish family with a beautiful 14-year-old son, Tadzio, with whom Aschenbach becomes obsessed. Unable to tear himself away, he remains in Venice despite an impending cholera epidemic and dies in his deckchair while watching the boy on the beach.

That is Thomas Mann's most famous story, *Death in Venice* (1912), in a nutshell. Such a brief description does no justice to the tragedy of Aschenbach's obsession, nor to the lushness of Mann's prose which relates it to us. On first setting eyes on Tadzio, Aschenbach 'noticed with astonishment that the boy was perfectly beautiful. His countenance…its evenly sloped nose, the lovely mouth, the expression of alluring and divine earnestness, was reminiscent of the noblest period of Greek sculpture.' Although his feelings ripen into sexual desire, they are sparked by an artistic appreciation of the boy's exquisiteness. The two occasionally exchange glances, but never speak: Aschenbach is not forced to confront his feelings and Tadzio does not lose his perfection. Yet we as readers feel all the older man's disgust at himself and the misery of a life lived without love.

WORKS TO READ
- *Buddenbrooks* (1901)
- *The Magic Mountain* (1924)
- *Joseph and his Brothers* (a four-volume retelling of stories from the book of Genesis, 1933–43)
- *Confessions of Felix Krull, Confidence Man* (1954)
- *Death in Venice and Other Stories* (1988 edition)

DID YOU KNOW?
The final opera written by Benjamin Britten, *Death in Venice* (1973), has the role of Tadzio played by a silent dancer, not a singer: as in Mann's story we never hear his voice. *Death in Venice* was at least partially based on Mann's own experience; he holidayed in Venice with his family in 1911 and finished the work in 1912.

The tone of *Death in Venice* is unremittingly melancholic; Mann's greatest novel, *The Magic Mountain* (1924), is philosophical and erudite; there are lighter moments to be found in *Buddenbrooks* (1901) and *Confessions of Felix Krull, Confidence Man* (1954). But all show the same meticulous attention to detail. From 'the coffin-black-varnished, black-upholstered chair' in the gondola in which Aschenbach arrives, to the over-ripe strawberries and the putrid scent of the lagoon, Mann records every sight, every sound, every sensation. When working on *Buddenbrooks*, the story of a wealthy merchant family strongly resembling his own, he wrote to relatives asking for recipes to be sure that he described meals accurately; in *Confessions of Felix Krull, Confidence Man*, the description of a delicatessen from which the young Felix stole sweets lasts for a page and a half and includes everything from hams and sausages to crayfish, caviar, foie gras and 'glass urns full of dessert chocolates and candied fruits'. But then, as Mann remarks in *The Magic Mountain*, 'We do not fear being called meticulous, inclining as we do to the view that only the exhaustive can be truly interesting.'

66

No one remains quite what he was when he recognizes himself.

99

The Magic Mountain, 1924

Buddenbrooks, 1901

GABRIEL GARCÍA MÁRQUEZ

COLOMBIAN
1927–2014

It's hard to overstate the impact of Gabriel García Márquez's *One Hundred Years of Solitude* (1967). It has been described as the most influential work written in Spanish since Miguel de Cervantes's *Don Quixote*, some three and a half centuries earlier. It brought Latin American literature to a worldwide audience and gave an identity not only to the author's native Colombia but also to a continent of hundreds of millions of people and a dozen nations. Its extraordinary first sentence, when Colonel Buendía, facing a firing squad, recalls the distant afternoon when his grandfather took him to discover ice, lures us into a mystery that, we can tell, will be lush, multi-layered and engrossing.

Márquez was brought up by a grandmother steeped in an oral tradition of ghosts and magic, in which the fantastical was commonplace; and by a grandfather who had fought in Colombia's civil war and who imbued his small grandson with a strong sense of his own country. As a result, the future writer developed a unique gift for combining the fabulous with the real and, working later as a journalist, believed that a writer should report what he saw, even if he saw it in his imagination. He wrote as if he were telling us stories that have been around since the beginning of time, that are both universal and personal.

Márquez's most prolific period – the 1960s to the 1980s – was a turbulent time in South America, with military dictatorships in many parts of the continent. Fervently

WORKS TO READ

In addition to those mentioned in the text:

- *The Autumn of the Patriarch* (1975)
- *Chronicle of a Death Foretold* (1981)
- *Collected Stories* (1984)
- *Of Love and Other Demons* (1994)
- *Memories of My Melancholy Whores* (2004)

DID YOU KNOW?

When Marquez died, the President of Columbia ordered three days of national mourning and asked that flags be flown at half-mast. Then-US President Barack Obama said the world had lost 'one of its greatest visionary writers', and added that he cherished a copy of *One Hundred Years of Solitude*, which Márquez had inscribed.

142

One Hundred Years of Solitude, 1967

>
>
> It is not true that people stop pursuing dreams because they grow old, they grow old because they stop pursuing dreams.
>
> "

left-wing, Márquez used metaphor and symbolism to express political points without risk of censorship: perhaps his single most important legacy was to show that no amount of oppression could limit the power of the human imagination.

Márquez was far from being a one-hit wonder. Before *One Hundred Years of Solitude*, he had aroused interest with *Leaf Storm* (1955) and tugged heartstrings with *No One Writes to the Colonel* (1961). Of his impressive array of later works, *Love in* the *Time of Cholera* (1985), questioning the conventional definition of true love, and *The General in his Labyrinth* (1989), an imagining of the last days of national hero Simón Bolívar, stand out; his childhood memoir *Living to Tell the Tale* (2002) is both an enchanting story and a fascinating insight into the influences that formed the author described as 'the most important Colombian who has ever lived'.

Love in the Time of Cholera, 1985

Gabriel García Márquez

El amor
en los tiempos
del cólera

YUKIO
MISHIMA

JAPANESE
1925–70

In November 1970 Yukio Mishima was the most famous literary figure in Japan, his autobiographical novel *Confessions of a Mask* (1949) having made him a literary celebrity at the age of 24. In addition to publishing vast numbers of novels, plays and short stories, he was a celebrated film actor and director, and a prominent right-wing activist. A staunch supporter of Japan's imperial system of government, he had even established his own private army, the Tatenokai, or 'shield society', with a view to overthrowing the constitution imposed on his country by the US at the end of World War II. On 25 November he and a handful of his followers marched into the army headquarters in Tokyo and, from its balcony, he addressed the garrison, urging them to revolt. When his audience jeered at him, he retreated inside and committed suicide, ritually disembowelling himself with his samurai sword.

It was clearly a political act, but also an artistic one: Mishima had been planning it for several years. Obsessed with the concept of physical beauty, he had said publicly and frequently that there was nothing uglier than old people; and he had left a note for his wife saying, 'Human life is limited, but I would like to live forever.'

Brought up by an ailing and eccentric grandmother and denied friends of his own age, the young Mishima had taken refuge in books, notably the macabre fairy tales of Hans Christian Andersen, and from an early age shut himself away in order to write. His

WORKS TO READ
- *Confessions of a Mask* (1949)
- *The Temple of the Golden Pavilion* (1956)
- *Kyoko's House* (1959)
- The *Sea of Fertility* tetralogy:
  Spring Snow (1969),
  Runaway Horses (1969),
  The Temple of Dawn (1970) and
  The Decay of the Angel (1971)

DID YOU KNOW?
Mishima was influenced by the way of life of the samurai warrior caste and wrote his own take on how their traditional practices and ethics related to modern Japanese life. He was profoundly unhappy with Westernization in his country, as he believed it corrupted and eroded the traditional identity of Japan.

146

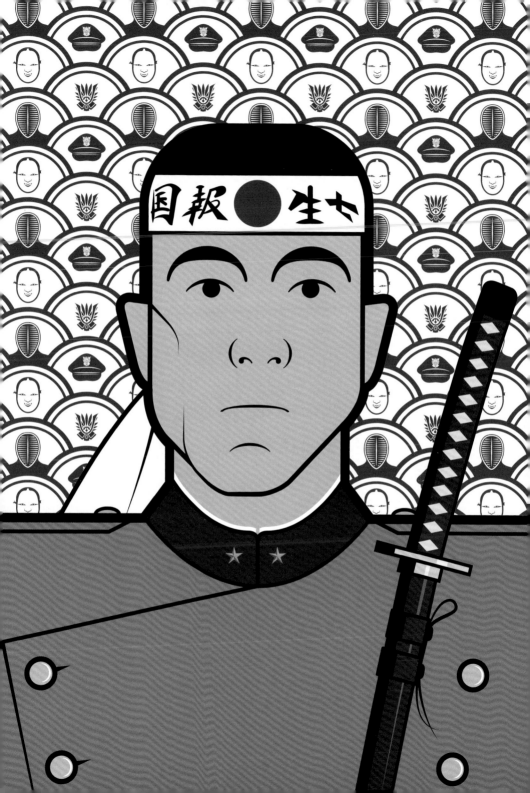

VINTAGE **MISHIMA**

Spring Snow

> 66
>
> I still have no way to survive but to keep writing one line.
>
> 99

Spring Snow, 1969

crowning achievement is probably *The Temple of the Golden Pavilion* (1956), in which the temple of the title is so beautiful that the protagonist feels that he cannot survive in its presence. Mishima also wrote plays for both Noh and Kabuki theatre, describing Noh as a tradition of 'exquisite refinement'. Naturally small and puny, he took up boxing and martial arts and built himself a magnificent – and much photographed – physique.

But his inner life seems to have been infested by self-loathing, sadomasochism and unhappiness with his probable homosexuality. The posthumously published *The Decay of the Angel* (1971) – the last volume of the *Sea of Fertility* tetralogy – has been seen as a negative assessment of his own achievements and a reiteration of his fear of old age. Public reaction to the manner of his death was angry and disapproving. As a friend said afterwards, 'He wanted to dramatize the end of his life in a beautiful way, but it was an over-elaborate gesture.'

Mishima speaking at Tokyo's military garrison station the day he died.

TONI
MORRISON

AMERICAN
BORN 1931

When she was about ten years old, Toni Morrison was discussing with a friend whether or not God existed. 'He doesn't,' said the friend. 'I've been praying for two years for him to give me blue eyes and he hasn't done it.' This girl, Morrison remembered years later, was beautiful. But they were living in a mixed-race community where blue eyes and blonde hair were considered essential for beauty, and the lovely young black girl was desperate to be other than she was.

This anecdote inspired Morrison's first novel, *The Bluest Eye* (1970). She recalled later that her friend's experience was a story she wanted to read, but no one was writing about that sort of thing – so she wrote it herself. Throughout her career, she has focused on chronicling the history of African-Americans, and in particular the injustices facing black American women.

Morrison's novels often make uncomfortable reading. The best-known, *Beloved* (1987), based on a true story, concerns a runaway slave named Sethe, who kills her own child rather than risk her being recaptured and returned to a life of bondage. Years later, a young woman calling herself Beloved (the only word that appears on the dead child's gravestone) inveigles her way into Sethe's home. Whether or not she is the ghost of the dead child, she comes to be seen as a spirit that needs to be exorcized. The tone throughout – as in all Morrison's work – is non-judgemental. No one, she

WORKS TO READ

- *The Bluest Eye* (1970)
- *Song of Solomon* (1977)
- *Beloved* (1987)
- *Love* (2003)
- *Home* (2012)

DID YOU KNOW?

The first black woman to win the Nobel Prize in Literature was born Chloe Ardelia Wofford. While the name Toni is often reported to come from her middle name Anthony, her birth certificate shows she was named Ardelia. Aged 12 she converted to Catholicism and was given the baptismal name Anthony, subsequently Toni.

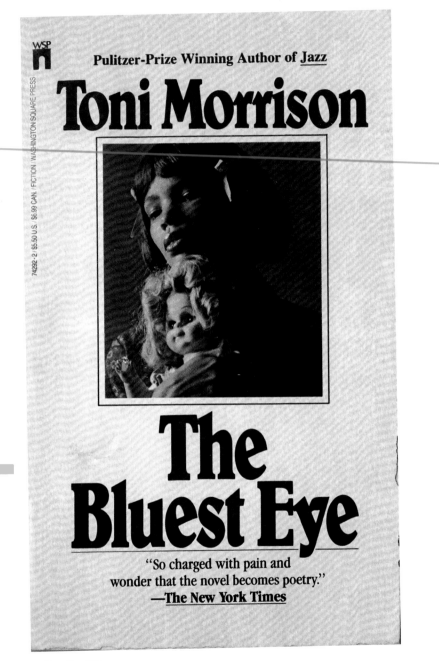

Toni Morrison

The Bluest Eye

"So charged with pain and
wonder that the novel becomes poetry."
—**The New York Times**

The Bluest Eye, 1970

says, has the right to judge Sethe except the dead child herself. But, although we may have powerful memories of dead loved ones, they sometimes need to be pushed aside in order for us to move on. This is, in part, a metaphor for a former slave's need to suppress the humiliation of being a slave if she is to get on with her life.

Speaking of a later novel, *Love* (2003), Morrison maintained the non-judgemental stance. Although it deals with the politics of race and class, and with a middle-aged man who marries an 11-year-old girl, another of its themes is reconciliation: the things people have to do, and the things they have to forget, if they are to live harmoniously together. Civil rights cannot achieve everything, Morrison tells us: we need love and humanity, too.

Morrison in New York City in 1979

IRIS
MURDOCH

IRISH
1919–99

It is a tragedy and an irony that Iris Murdoch should be best remembered (through the film *Iris*, directed by Richard Eyre, 2001, based on her husband John Bayley's memoir) for having suffered from Alzheimer's; she was, in fact, one of the most intelligent and profoundly thoughtful novelists of her generation.

Murdoch studied Greats (Classics) at Oxford and philosophy as a postgraduate at Cambridge, then wrote about and lectured in philosophy before devoting herself to fiction. Although she denied being a philosophical novelist, her characters are always facing ethical dilemmas, very often because they have fallen obsessively in love with somebody unsuitable, unresponsive and/or married. According to her friend and fellow novelist Malcolm Bradbury, Murdoch saw the novel as an instrument for dealing with ideas. As she herself put it, 'Life is very terrible and very funny'; she wanted to convey 'the unique strangeness of human beings'.

She achieved fame with early novels such as *The Bell* (1958), the bell of the title belonging to an ancient abbey and representing the need for spirituality in a secular world. Notoriety followed with *A Severed Head* (1961), which featured castration and incest as well as adultery. Real critical success came with *An Accidental Man* (1971), with its complex network of unfulfilled relationships and changing partners, and *The Black Prince* (1973), in which the narrative is 'topped and tailed' with additions

WORKS TO READ
- *The Bell* (1958)
- *An Accidental Man* (1971)
- *The Black Prince* (1973)
- *The Sacred and Profane Love Machine* (1974)
- *The Sea, the Sea* (1978)

DID YOU KNOW?
In 1946 Iris Murdoch won a scholarship to study at Vassar College, New York, but was refused a visa to the US as, when studying at Oxford, she had joined the Communist Party of Great Britain. Although she later left the party and was allowed entry to the US, she always had to obtain special permission.

VINTAGE **MURDOCH**

The *B*ell

by four characters commenting on the central character's version of events. Then came *The Sacred and Profane Love Machine* (1974), another study of adultery, and Booker Prize-winning *The Sea, the Sea* (1978), in which the self-centred (and clearly unreliable) narrator re-encounters the woman he was in love with decades ago and becomes obsessed with her all over again.

Murdoch's critics have often complained about the lushness of her prose and her notorious overuse of adjectives: 'closely covered with millions of tiny sharp broken-off limpet shells' (from *The Sea, the Sea*) is typical. Fans, on the other hand, revel in her attention to detail and her masterly handling of complex plots. Neither group can deny that you come away from an Iris Murdoch novel pondering the problems of freedom and your obligations to other people: the difficulties of trying to be a good person.

Murdoch at home, 1960

VLADIMIR NABOKOV

Russian-
American
1899–1977

Born in St Petersburg into a wealthy aristocratic family, Vladimir Nabokov lost everything during the 1917 Revolution, fled from Russia and lived the rest of his life in one form of exile or another. He studied in England, then moved to Berlin and later, because his wife was Jewish, to Paris and the US as the Nazis gained power in Germany. Even when the success of his masterpiece *Lolita* (1955) made him rich, he chose not to buy a home but to reside for the last 16 years of his life in the luxurious Montreux Palace Hotel in Switzerland.

His first nine novels, written in Russian, evoke a sense of loss and nostalgia for a Russia that no longer exists. They include *Mary* (1926), set in a gloomy boarding house for émigrés in Berlin, and *The Luzhin Defense* (sometimes entitled *The Defense*; 1930), about a chess champion driven to insanity by his obsession with the game.

Obsession was a feature of many Nabokov novels: never more so than in *Lolita*. In it, the narrator, Humbert Humbert, a professor of literature in his late 30s, becomes so infatuated with his landlady's 12-year-old daughter that he marries the mother just to be near the girl. When the mother is killed in a road accident, he travels with Lolita from seedy motel to seedy motel across the US, plagued by guilt and paranoia. Later, while he is in prison after committing a serious crime, Humbert writes the memoir/confession that becomes *Lolita*.

WORKS TO READ

- *Mary* (1926)
- *The Luzhin Defense* (1930)
- *Bend Sinister* (1947)
- *Lolita* (1955)
- *Ada, or Ardor: A Family Chronicle* (1969)

DID YOU KNOW?

Nabokov was a self-taught expert lepidopterist and has a genus of butterflies (*Nabakovia*) named after him. He inherited his interest from his parents. When he was a child, his father was arrested for his political activities and the eight-year-old Vladimir Nabokov took a butterfly to his cell as a present.

Humbert is an extraordinary character: cynical yet prey to an uncontrollable passion; conceited yet self-abasing. He revels in Lolita's innocence, yet describes girls like her as revealing their true 'demoniac' nature to 'certain bewitched travellers, twice or many times older than they'. Nabokov leaves it to the reader to decide just how aware of her sexual power Lolita is, and to what extent Humbert is a pervert, a victim or even, in the end, the hero of a tragic love story. The author himself denied that he had any moral message; he liked posing riddles and finding elegant solutions for them.

Nabokov once described the Russian language as 'untrammelled, infinitely rich', and regretted having to abandon it for English. No one reading *Lolita* can fail to recognize that in his adopted tongue he had found something equally untrammelled and infinitely rich.

Page from *Poems and Verses*, inscribed to Nabokov's wife, Vera, in 1948 and 1969

Vladimir Nabokov

Lolita

The greatest novel of rapture in modern fiction

R K
NARAYAN

INDIAN
1906–2001

In the unremarkable southern Indian town of Malgudi live Srinivas, the editor of the weekly newspaper (*Mr Sampath*, 1948); Railway Raju, the smooth-talking tourist guide turned reluctant spiritual leader (*The Guide*, 1958); Vasu, the taxidermist (*The Man-Eater of Malgudi*, 1961); and many more. R K Narayan used this fictional setting for most of his novels and stories, and it teems with life, gentle conflict, humour and understated morality.

One of the first prominent Indian novelists to write in English, Narayan introduced a generation of Western readers to India and Indian life. Critics have said that his work is too benign: the six decades during which he was writing saw the great upheavals of independence and partition, violence and horrific poverty, but these are for the most part faint murmurings in the background of Malgudi life. Most of Narayan's characters are Hindu, so there is no undercurrent of religious conflict. They live simply, but they have homes and a servant and can afford to send their children to school.

It's unfair to say that Narayan entirely ignored the outside world: Mahatma Gandhi and the Quit India Movement of 1942 take centre stage in *Waiting for the Mahatma* (1955), while in *The Painter of Signs* (1977) the calligrapher Raman shocks the locals by producing signboards for an office promoting family planning. The novels have also been described as deeply religious: the Hindu concept of *dharma* – a complicated mix

WORKS TO READ
- *Swami and Friends* (1935)
- *Malgudi Days* (short stories, 1942)
- *Waiting for the Mahatma* (1955)
- *The Guide* (1958)
- *The Man-Eater of Malgudi* (1961)

DID YOU KNOW?
R K Narayan decided early in his career to quit teaching and write. His first published work was not a novel, but a book review of *Development of Maritime Laws of 17th-Century England*. He won various awards and was nominated twice for the Nobel Prize, although he never won it.

> **66**
>
> You become writer by writing. It is a yoga.
>
> **99**

The Guide, 1958

of duty and moral and natural law – flows through them, as characters' innate flaws and vices lead them into trouble.

What critics tend to overlook, however, is just how funny Narayan is. In *Swami and Friends* (1935) a schoolboy observes that 'if he were Swaminathan, he would have closed the whole incident at the beginning by hurling an ink-bottle, if nothing bigger was available, at the teacher'. Railway Raju, accidentally and cynically becoming a tour guide, remarks of a client, 'It seemed to me silly to go a hundred miles to see the source of [the river] Sarayu when it had taken the trouble to tumble down the mountain and come to our door…but the man who had gone was all praise for the spot.' Those who don't choose to delve deeper may enjoy Narayan at face value, as a gentle satirist on the human condition and the self-delusion in which we all indulge sometimes.

O

TO

R

ORWELL
PROUST
RUSHDIE

GEORGE
ORWELL

BRITISH
1903–50

A bit like Franz KAFKA, George Orwell's name and work have made their mark even on those who haven't read his writings: we know that Big Brother is watching us, that Room 101 contains terrible things and that our brains can be distorted by Newspeak and doublethink.

These are all concepts from Orwell's dystopian novel *Nineteen Eighty-Four* (1949), with its dire warnings against the evils of the totalitarian state. His other politically inspired novel, *Animal Farm* (1945) – in which the animals oust the drunken farmer, take over the farm and then fall out among themselves – is an allegory of events following the Russian Revolution of 1917 and in particular a denunciation of Stalinism. Although a lifelong Socialist, Orwell had no sympathy with the extremism into which he felt Russia had fallen.

Orwell was born in India, educated at Eton (on a scholarship – his background was not wealthy), then served in the Indian Imperial Police in Burma. Appalled by Imperialism, he resigned in 1927, spent some time in poverty, then turned to writing and, in 1936, went to Spain to fight against Fascism. These experiences inspired his first novel, *Burmese Days* (1934), and three powerful pieces of memoir/journalism: *Down and Out in Paris and London* (1933), *The Road to Wigan Pier* (1937) and his masterly analysis of the Spanish Civil War, *Homage to Catalonia* (1938). He also

WORKS TO READ

- *Down and Out in Paris and London* (1933)
- *Homage to Catalonia* (1938)
- *Animal Farm* (1945)
- *Nineteen Eighty-Four* (1949)
- *Why I Write* (2004, a collection of essays including 'Politics and the English Language')

DID YOU KNOW?

Orwell's real name was Eric Blair. He published *Down and Out in Paris and London* under a pseudonym so as not to embarrass his family with its content, choosing George Orwell because he was living near the River Orwell in Suffolk and because it was 'a good round English name'.

wrote a number of novels satirizing English middle-class life and containing a note of subversion that presages *Nineteen Eighty-Four*. Perhaps the best of these is *Keep the Aspidistra Flying* (1936), though its protagonist is rebelling not against Big Brother but against the Money God that forces him (like his author at one time) to scrape a living in a bookshop.

Orwell made a point of writing clear, precise and unpretentious English: one of his maxims was 'Never use a long word if a short one will do.' But, he felt, there was more to it than that. In an essay entitled *'Politics and the English Language'* (1946), he warned against the dangers of careless writing generally, and added – again foreshadowing his most famous work – 'Political language…is designed to make lies sound truthful and murder respectable, and to give an appearance of solidity to pure wind.'

In another parallel with Franz Kafka, Orwell suffered from poor health for most of his life and died of tuberculosis while he was only in his 40s.

During times of universal deceit, telling the truth becomes a revolutionary act.

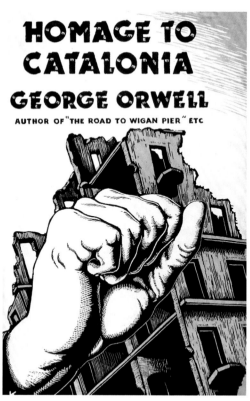

Homage to Catalonia, 1938

Animal Farm, 1945

Penguin Modern Classics

2/6

George Orwell

Animal Farm

MARCEL PROUST

FRENCH
1871–1922

'Well, it isn't Proust,' we say, of any writing that somehow falls short of the ideal, and no other writer in this book was so tirelessly, passionately, obsessively determined to make every word perfect, every description precise, every insight into art, society and humanity as penetrating as it could possibly be.

Marcel Proust's masterwork – indeed his only substantial work – *In Search of Lost Time*, was published in seven volumes between 1913 and 1927 and has been described (in competition with James JOYCE's *Ulysses*, 1922) as the greatest novel of the 20th century. Superficially, it is a fictionalized autobiography, but its theme is the important role that memory – involuntary memory, memory we don't know we possess – plays in all our lives. The tiniest incident – tripping over an uneven cobblestone, wiping one's mouth with a starched napkin, trying not to rattle a teaspoon in a saucer – recalls 'lost time' and enables the author (whom we are told we may call Marcel) to understand his past more clearly.

Painstaking analysis of the feelings that these tiny incidents produce is the hallmark of Proust's style. The famous incident of eating a morsel of madeleine dunked in tea fills him with 'all-powerful joy', making him cease to feel 'mediocre, accidental, mortal'; he later devotes several pages to the scent and sight of hawthorn blossom, unable to pinpoint or to convey to his satisfaction the feelings that it arouses in him.

WORKS TO READ

- *In Search of Lost Time* volumes 1–7:
  Swann's Way (1913)
  In the Shadow of Young Girls in Flower (1919)
  'The Guermantes Way' (1920–1)
  Sodom and Gomorrah (1921–2)
  The Prisoner (1923)
  The Fugitive (1925)
  Time Regained (1927)

DID YOU KNOW?

Proust based the town of Combray, where Marcel spent his formative childhood holidays, on Illiers in northern France. His father was born in Illiers and his aunt Elisabeth married a local notable, whose house has now been converted into the Marcel Proust Museum. In 1971, to honour the centennial of Proust's birth, the town was renamed Illiers-Combray.

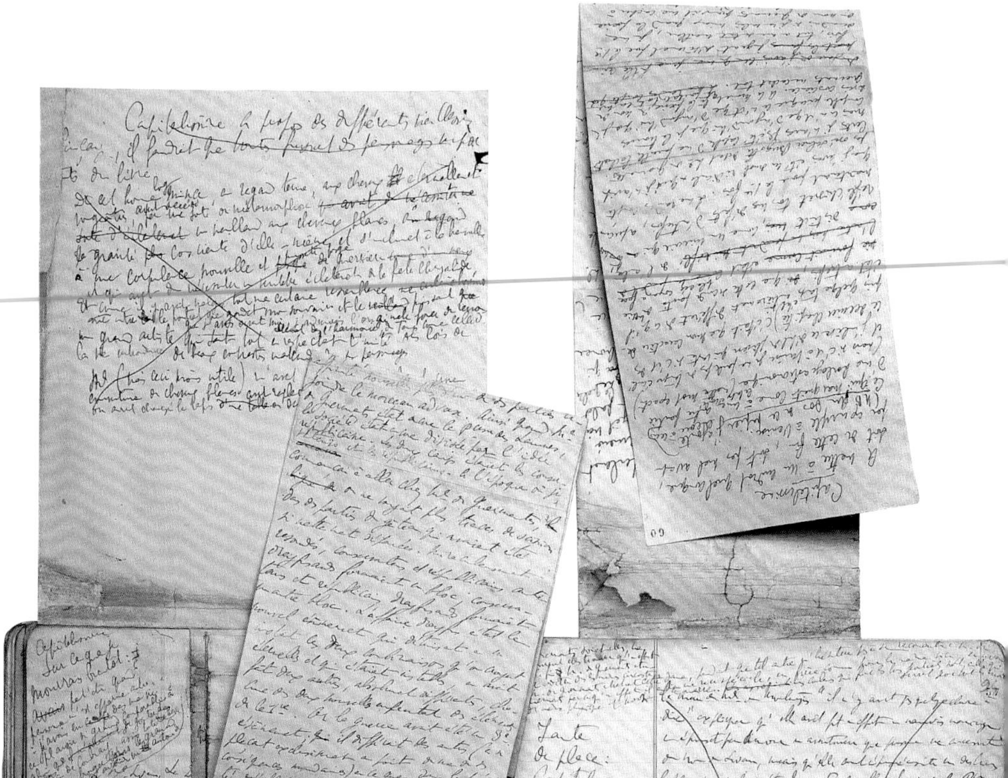

> Everything great in the world comes from neurotics. They alone have founded our religions and composed our masterpieces.

These are both incidents from Marcel's childhood; later, he is similarly obsessive about his love affairs and about Paris high society as World War I brings the *belle époque* crashing to its knees. But more than anything Marcel is interested in art: he reverts again and again to the idea that only art is real, pure, true. When he finally decides to embark on the novel he has intended to write for so long, it is because he has at last understood 'that all the materials of a work of literature were simply my past life…I had stored them up without divining the purpose for which they were intended'.

For Proust, memory, art and life are inextricably intertwined and no one who reads him will ever look at a madeleine or a hawthorn the same way again.

Proust c. 1896

Selection of Proust's pages from *In Search of Lost Time* (1913–27)

SALMAN RUSHDIE

BRITISH–
INDIAN
BORN 1947

Born in Mumbai just eight weeks before India became an independent nation, Salman Rushdie grew up hand in hand with his newborn country. This coincidence later inspired *Midnight's Children* (1981), which not only won the Booker Prize in 1981, but in 2008 was also voted by the public the best novel in the prize's 40-year history.

The central character, Saleem Sinai, is born at exactly midnight on 15 August 1947, the very moment when independent India comes into being. Within an hour, a thousand more babies are born, all endowed with special powers – they are the 'midnight's children' of the title. Saleem's story parallels the tangled history of the emerging India, with themes of disappointed hopes, arguable choices and directions not taken. The magical elements of the book have led to its being dubbed 'magical realism', while the vast cast of larger-than-life characters, the humour and the throbbing identity of Mumbai itself have drawn parallels with *David Copperfield* (1870) and Dickensian London.

Midnight's Children brought Rushdie critical and popular recognition; his fourth novel, *The Satanic Verses* (1988), so offended parts of the Muslim community that the Ayatollah Khomeini, who was then the spiritual and political leader of Iran, issued a fatwa demanding the author's execution on the grounds of blasphemy. As a result, Rushdie lived in hiding for a number of years. The controversy overshadowed the

WORKS TO READ

- *Midnight's Children* (1981)
- *Shame* (1983)
- *The Moor's Last Sigh* (1995)
- *Joseph Anton* (2012)
- *Two Years Eight Months & Twenty-Eight Nights* (2015)

DID YOU KNOW?

Rushdie's time in hiding amounted to ten years after the fatwa was issued against him. In 1990 he publicly announced a return to Islam, although when this didn't stop the death threats he later admitted it had been for show.

book itself, which is based in part on the life of Mohammed and uses a similar blend of history and magical realism to *Midnight's Children*.

Rushdie's other work includes *Shame* (1983), set against a background of political turmoil in Pakistan; *The Moor's Last Sigh* (1995), a magical-realist family saga; and *Two Years Eight Months and Twenty-Eight Nights* (2015), a mix of history and myth set in the near future. The nights in the title add up to one thousand and one, which, like the thousand and one babies of *Midnight's Children*, is a conscious reference to the tales of Scheherezade. Rushdie has also written short stories (*East, West*, 1994) and books for children (*Haroun and the Sea of Stories*, 1990; *Luka and the Fire of Life*, 2010). In 2012 he published a memoir of his time under police protection: its title, *Joseph Anton*, is the codename he took in those years, a tribute to two of his favourite authors, Joseph Conrad and Anton Chekhov.

A poet's work is to name the unnameable, to point at frauds, to take sides, start arguments, shape the world, and stop it going to sleep.

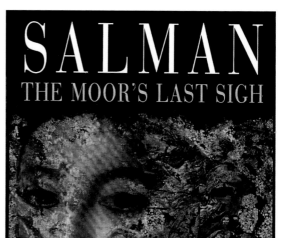

The Moor's Last Sigh, 1995

S

TO

T

**SALINGER
SARTRE
SOLZHENITSYN
STEINBECK
THOMAS**

J D
SALINGER

AMERICAN
1919–2010

'If you really want to hear about it, the first thing you'll probably want to know is where I was born, and what my lousy childhood was like…and all that David Copperfield kind of crap…'

In 1951, when *The Catcher in the Rye* was published, the word 'teenager' was a recent coinage and the publishing genre 'Young Adult' was unheard of. The disenchanted voice of 16-year-old Holden Caulfield delighted young people and shocked their parents everywhere.

Holden, about to be expelled from school, decides to return home to New York without telling his parents and spend a few unrestricted days in the city. After various uncomfortable meetings with old friends and new acquaintances, as well as several failed attempts at sexual encounters, he sneaks into his parents' apartment at night to wake the only person with whom he seems to have a rapport, his younger sister Phoebe. The novel ends with an eye-opening outing with Phoebe to the carousel in Central Park, followed by a scene showing Holden uncertain what the future holds for him: 'How do you know what you're going to do till you *do* it?…I swear it's a stupid question.'

Jerome David Salinger's only full-length novel was controversial from the moment it appeared. Critics decried its casual and sometimes coarse language; fans loved it for

WORKS TO READ

- *The Catcher in the Rye* (1951)
- *Franny and Zooey*
  (published as separate stories in 1955 and 1957 and in a single volume in 1961)
- *Raise High the Roof Beam, Carpenters* and *Seymour: An Introduction* (published in a single volume in 1963)

DID YOU KNOW?

The title *The Catcher in the Rye* comes from Holden's idea that that is what he'd like to be – a catcher in a field of rye, saving children who are about to fall over a cliff. Holden details his vocational fantasy to his younger sister Phoebe, as to rescue children (particularly his sister) from the phoniness of the adult world is a prevailing preoccupation.

Salinger in 1953

> 66
>
> There's no more to Holden Caulfield. Read the book again. It's all there. Holden Caulfield is only a frozen moment in time.
>
> 99

the same reasons, and because for the first time a work of literature had attempted to get inside a teenager's head – and succeeded triumphantly.

The Catcher in the Rye is not Salinger's only achievement. His stories about the fictional Glass family, notably 'Raise High the Roof Beam, Carpenters' (1955) and 'Seymour: An Introduction' (1959), are understated and unsung masterpieces. Narrated by Buddy Glass and remembering an elder brother who has committed suicide, they are so realistic, so full of detail (such as the way Seymour's hair used to land all over Buddy when they went to the barber's together) and so touching that it is hard to remember that they are works of fiction, not genuine memoirs.

Disliking the attention that *The Catcher in the Rye* brought him, Salinger became very reclusive and fought several legal battles with those who sought to invade his privacy. If anything, this added to his mystique, giving him cult status with the many who believed that Holden Caulfield was one of the great young voices of his – or any other – generation.

The Catcher in the Rye, 1951

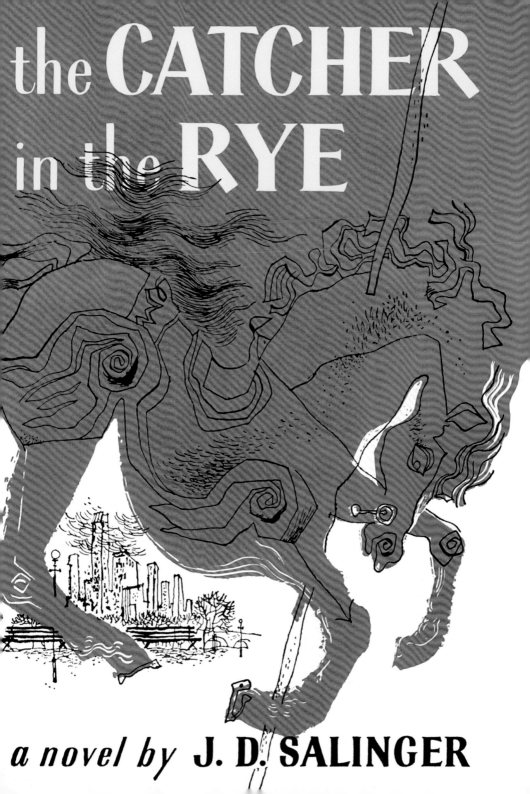

the CATCHER in the RYE

a novel by **J. D. SALINGER**

JEAN-PAUL SARTRE

FRENCH

1905–80

'Existence precedes essence,' said Jean-Paul Sartre as part of his definition of the philosophy of existentialism. Put more simply, there is no blueprint for a human being: everything we are, everything we do is the result of our own choice. Even not choosing is a choice. We are, as he rather gloomily put it, 'condemned to be free'.

Born in Paris into an intellectual bourgeois family, Sartre became the centre of Left Bank café society, surrounded by left-wing writers, artists and jazz musicians, including long-term lover Simone de BEAUVOIR. He first attracted literary attention with his philosophical novel *Nausea* (1938), about a man trying to write a biography of an 18th-century aristocrat finding that the more he researches, the less he is able to get a handle on his subject. Sartre's view was that trying to tell a life story, whether one's own or someone else's, with a beginning, a middle and an end, was doomed to failure. Ourselves, he said, are not what we perceive, but a reflection of how others perceive us.

Captured by the Germans in 1940, he spent time as a prisoner of war and wrote two of his most successful plays during the Nazi occupation. *The Flies* (1943) uses a classical Greek subject to explore the theme of liberation, while *Huis Clos* (variously translated as *In Camera, Behind Closed Doors* and *No Exit*, 1944) shows three people locked in the same room in Hell, condemned to spend eternity with each other; it contains Sartre's famous *bon mot:* 'Hell is other people.'

WORKS TO READ

- *Nausea* (1938)
- *Being and Nothingness* (philosophy, 1943)
- *Huis Clos* (play, 1944)
- *The Roads to Freedom* tetralogy (1945–9)
- *Critique of Dialectical Reason* (philosophy, 1960)

DID YOU KNOW?

Sartre is the only person voluntarily to have declined the Nobel Prize in Literature. He also declined the highest French accolade, the *Légion d'honneur,* after World War II. Sartre explained that he always declined official honours, no matter how honourable the circumstances, for fear of being institutionalized.

After the war, Sartre founded the political and literary magazine *Les Temps Modernes* with the purpose of publishing *littérature engagée* – literature that was politically and socially committed. He also wrote the *Roads to Freedom* trilogy (1945–49), a similarly 'engaged' work in which the central character, Mathieu, has to make moral decisions about both his personal and his political life.

Later in life Sartre devoted himself more to politics and philosophy than to the writing of fiction. His great legacy is that his philosophy is inextricably linked to ethics and to human consciousness: he shows how grand ideas are relevant to the way each and every one of us behaves.

Sartre in May 1968

No Exit, 1944

ALEKSANDR
SOLZHENITSYN

RUSSIAN
1918–2008

There can't be many writers who can claim to have brought down a regime more or less single-handedly, but Aleksandr Solzhenitsyn would be one of them. His exposés of conditions inside Soviet labour camps sowed seeds of dissatisfaction among the Russian people that eventually led to the break-up of the USSR in 1991.

Solzhenitsyn had espoused both atheism and Marxism at school but, serving in the army during World War II, he became disillusioned with Joseph Stalin, who he believed had corrupted the Communist ideals of Karl Marx and Vladimir Lenin. Letters in which he confided these indiscreet opinions to a friend were intercepted by the authorities, and in 1945 he was arrested and sentenced to eight years in a 'corrective' labour camp, followed by exile in Kazakhstan.

These experiences inspired his most influential books. Nine years after his release, *One Day in the Life of Ivan Denisovich* (1962) was published with the express permission of the comparatively liberal Soviet leader Nikita Khrushchev. Encapsulating, as Solzhenitsyn put it, 'the entire camp in a drop of water', it showed the hardships and cruelties the inmates suffered. Nothing like this had ever been published legally in the Soviet Union before. It was a literary and political sensation across the world.

Two years later Khrushchev fell from power and a more restrictive regime prevented publication in Russia of Solzhenitsyn's next novels: *The First Circle* (based on his

WORKS TO READ

- *One Day in the Life of Ivan Denisovich* (1962)
- *The First Circle* (1968)
- *Cancer Ward* (1968)
- *The Gulag Archipelago* (1973)
- *The Red Wheel* (1971–91)

DID YOU KNOW?

While in prison, Solzhenitsyn composed some 8,000 poems in his head or on scraps of paper that he threw away when he had committed them to memory. He chose poetry because it is easier to memorize than prose. 'Prussian Nights', about 12,000 lines and more than 50 pages long, was one such poem.

Anyone who has proclaimed violence his method inexorably must choose lying as his principle.

Solzhenitsky on his release from the gulag, March 1953

experiences working in a research institute while a prisoner) and *Cancer Ward* (inspired by his own treatment for cancer) were eventually published abroad in 1968. He went back to writing in secret, hiding his manuscripts and smuggling them out of the country on microfilm. But the floodgates had been opened: hundreds of former inmates of the camps sent him their reminiscences, which he combined with his own memories and research to produce *The Gulag Archipelago* (1973).

International uproar followed when this massive history/memoir was published in Paris. Solzhenitsyn was exiled and stripped of Russian citizenship. For most of the next 20 years he lived in the US, working on a series of novels about the Russian Revolution, *The Red Wheel* (1971–91).

The collapse of the Soviet Union in 1991 enabled him to return 'home'. Permitted to travel and to express political opinions, he remained faithful to his determination to tell the truth – the whole truth – in everything he wrote and said.

The Gulag Archipelago, 1973

JOHN STEINBECK

AMERICAN
1902–68

During the 1930s, economic and environmental disasters drove some half-million farm workers to leave their homes in Oklahoma, Arkansas and other Midwestern states and travel west in the hope of finding employment. Small-scale farming had become uneconomical, banks were foreclosing and an exodus of biblical proportions took place along Route 66 – 'the road of flight' – as the 20th-century equivalent of the Children of Israel headed in desperation for the Promised Land of California.

Unfortunately, the Californians didn't see it that way. State borders were closed to migrants who didn't have jobs, even though they were US citizens. Those who did get through lived in appalling conditions in labour camps where exploitation, below-subsistence wages and malnutrition were commonplace.

It was against this background that John Steinbeck's writing career blossomed. Born and raised in comfortable circumstances in Salinas, California, he had seen the plight of migrant agricultural workers from an early age. He wrote about them humorously in *Tortilla Flat* (1935), neutrally in *In Dubious Battle* (1936) and compassionately in *Of Mice and Men* (1937). But by the time he came to write his masterpiece, *The Grapes of Wrath* (1939), he knew about conditions in the labour camps and he was angry. The story of a family of refugees from Oklahoma, *The Grapes of Wrath* was a bestseller and brought the migrants' hardships to a vastly wider audience, shocking

WORKS TO READ

- *Tortilla Flat* (1935)
- *Of Mice and Men* (1937)
- *The Grapes of Wrath* (1939)
- *Cannery Row* (1945)
- *East of Eden* (1952)

DID YOU KNOW?

Steinbeck liked to write in graphite pencils and could go through as many as 60 a day. *East of Eden* took a year to write and, according to Steinbeck's records, 25 dozen pencils and about 36 reams of paper. He had developed a callus by the time the book was finished.

Cannery Row film adaptation (David S Ward), 1982

many with its 'earthy' language. The book was widely banned and burned, and led to Steinbeck's being branded a Communist, an inaccurate label he never quite shook off.

Steinbeck had studied marine biology and was ahead of his time in seeing humanity as a microcosm in the greater ecosystem of life. 'It is advisable to look from the tide pool to the stars and then back to the tide pool again,' he wrote. *Cannery Row* (1945), with its assorted community of biologists, layabouts and whores, portrayed just such a microcosm, while the massive *East of Eden* (1952) used the author's own background to express universal truths about family life.

Steinbeck was never part of the American literary establishment: even when he won the Nobel Prize in Literature in 1962, he was seen as too proletarian, having 'too much dirt under his fingernails'. Yet, as the British broadcaster Melvyn Bragg memorably remarked in a 2011 BBC documentary devoted to *John Steinbeck: The Voice of America*, he wrote at least four masterpieces – 'four more than the vast majority of writers ever manage to do'.

The Grapes of Wrath, 1939

DYLAN THOMAS

WELSH

1914-53

'To begin at the beginning:

It is Spring, moonless night in the small town…'

Thus, lyrically, begins Dylan Thomas's most famous work, the 'play for voices' *Under Milk Wood* (1954). Unfinished at the time of his death, it recounts a day in the lives, loves and dreams of the people of Llareggub, a fictional small seaside town in his native Wales. A cast of memorable characters includes the obsessively house-proud Mrs Ogmore-Pritchard, who wants the sun to wipe its shoes before it is allowed in; Dai Bread, the bigamist baker; and Mr Pugh, the retired schoolmaster who longs to poison his wife ('Here's your arsenic, dear, and your weed-killer biscuit').

Thomas, described by one biographer as 'the finest lyric poet since Keats', was born in a Swansea suburb, where his father, a local schoolteacher, read great works of literature aloud to him long before the young Dylan was old enough to understand them. This early exposure to the beauty of language sparked Dylan's conviction that he was destined to be a poet. He wrote assiduously throughout his teens and published his first collection of poetry at the age of 20. He then moved to London, became part of the bohemian community and took to the drink that would dominate the rest of his life. When he met his future wife, Caitlin Macnamara, shortly afterwards, he already, she said, looked dishevelled and like 'a parody of a poet'. Long after his

WORKS TO READ

- *Portrait of the Artist as a Young Dog* (short stories, 1940)
- *A Child's Christmas in Wales* (prose pieces, 1952)
- *Collected Poems* (1953)
- *Under Milk Wood* (1954)

DID YOU KNOW?

Thomas's father chose the name Dylan, after Dylan ail Don, a character in *The Mabinogion*, the famous collection of Welsh folktales. Although his parents were bilingual in Welsh and English, Thomas was not, and favoured the anglicized pronunciation of the name Dylan over the Welsh (Dillan as opposed to Dullan).

death from pneumonia Caitlin remarked that Dylan had 'created a legend and then lived up to it'.

After their marriage in 1937 the Thomases returned to Wales, to the fishing village of Laugharne, although the need to earn money often took Dylan to London. His recordings for the BBC brought him fame but never fortune. London, however, inspired some of his best poetry: elegies to the victims of the Blitz, including the poignant and powerful 'A Refusal to Mourn the Death by Fire of a Child in London' (1946).

After the war, he began to tour the US, lecturing from coast to coast and wearing himself out with work and drink. In November 1953 he collapsed in New York after a whiskey-driven bender, went into a coma and died four days later. At the time, he was the most famous 20th-century poet of the English language.

Six months before his death, he had been directing the first public reading of *Under Milk Wood*. In an instruction that could have become his epitaph, he exhorted the cast, 'Love the words. Love the words.'

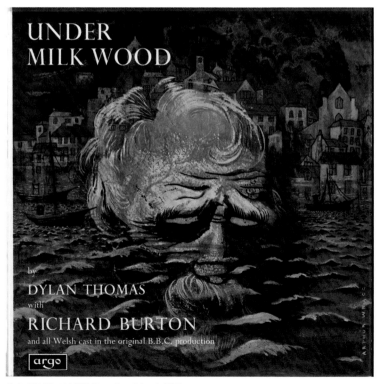

Under Milk Wood, 1954. Recording pictured, 1954.

U
TO
Z

UPDIKE
VONNEGUT
WOOLF
XUN
ZWEIG

JOHN UPDIKE

AMERICAN
1932–2009

When John Updike died, tributes described him as 'our time's greatest man of letters', 'the finest writer working in English' and 'one of the funniest and most acute observers of American life'. He was acclaimed not only as a novelist, but also as an essayist, poet and writer of short stories. Yet his subjects were modest: the small town, the failed marriage, the disappointing career and, most famously, in his four 'Rabbit' novels, the American Everyman, who by the end of the series is trying to be a father and grandfather 'with imperfect success but not entire failure'.

Harry 'Rabbit' Angstrom first appeared in *Rabbit, Run* (1960) as a former high school basketball star, now in his 20s, stuck in an unhappy marriage and a boring job. The nickname comes largely from his speed on the basketball court, but may also have something to do with his sexual proclivities: the difficulty of balancing sexual impulses against domestic stability recurs again and again in Updike's work.

Updike returned to his character at roughly ten-year intervals, in *Rabbit Redux* (1971), *Rabbit Is Rich* (1981) and *Rabbit at Rest* (1990). He said of life in small towns, 'We are not as dumb as you city people think,' and he used Rabbit to reflect on such issues as US involvement in the Vietnam War, the moon landings and the growing drug culture. A later novel, *In the Beauty of the Lilies* (1996), describes the lives of four generations of a family and considers the twin powers of the Church and the cinema

WORKS TO READ

- The *Rabbit* series (1971, 1981 and 1990)
- *The Witches of Eastwick* (1984)
- *In the Beauty of the Lilies* (1996)
- *The Complete Henry Bech* (novels and stories, 2001)
- *My Father's Tears and Other Stories* (2009)

DID YOU KNOW?

The American rapper Eminem is familiar with Updike's famous character Rabbit. Rabbit is the nickname of Eminem's character Jimmy in the film *8 Mile*, which also features the song 'Rabbit, Run'. The *8 Mile* screenplay opens with a line from Updike's novel, 'If you have the guts to be yourself ... other people'll pay your price.'

across the 20th century: as a child in the 1930s, Updike remembered, he had found the cinema the more uplifting of the two.

The Witches of Eastwick (1984), subsequently much staged and filmed, attracted some controversy: did it portray its female characters as being powerless without a man (even if that man turned out to be the Devil) or was it a satire on that attitude? Without answering the question, one critic speculated that Updike 'finds wickedness and mischief more engrossing as subjects than goodness and wisdom'.

As for his short stories, his final collection, *My Father's Tears and Other Stories* (2009), is a gem: it is full of a sense of waste, of youthful opportunities passed up and of the nearness of death, but every sentence, every description is perfectly crafted and touches the heart.

66

You cannot help but learn more as you take the world into your hands. Take it up reverently, for it is an old piece of clay, with millions of thumbprints on it.

99

Updike c. 1960

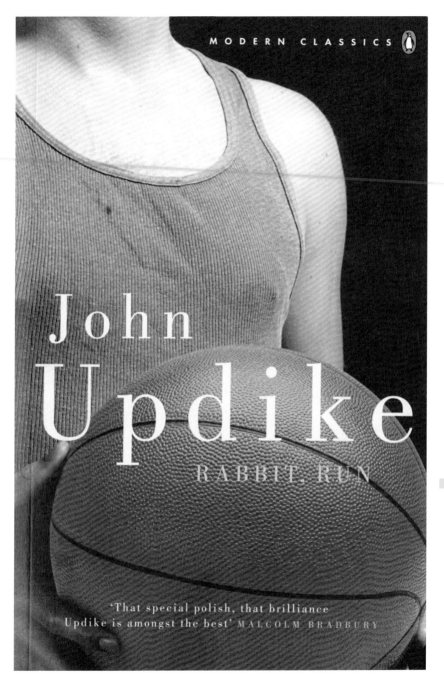

John
Updike

RABBIT, RUN

'That special polish, that brilliance
Updike is amongst the best' MALCOLM BRADBURY

Rabbit, Run, 1960

KURT
VONNEGUT

AMERICAN

1922–2007

In February 1945, aged 22, Kurt Vonnegut, an American prisoner of war in Dresden, Germany, witnessed the carpet-bombing of that city that killed at least 25,000 people. He later reported that he had been in an underground meat-locker making vitamin supplements when bombing began. When he emerged, death was all around him. It took 20 years and several failed attempts for him to write at length about this experience, but when eventually he succeeded the result was his most famous novel, *Slaughterhouse-Five* (1969).

The novel's hero, Billy Pilgrim (who has himself witnessed the destruction of Dresden), has become 'unstuck in time', so that he never knows what part of his life he is going to have to act in next. Not only that, but he has been kidnapped and taken by flying saucer to the planet Tralfamadore. Here he learns an entirely new attitude to time and realizes that death is just an unpleasant moment. Sadly, circumstances conspire to prevent him from sharing this wisdom with the world.

Vonnegut had been drawn to science fiction because he felt that while mainstream 'literary' writers were analysing human relationships, science fiction was confronting issues of grave importance to society. In *Slaughterhouse-Five* he said that he had used science fiction for 'relief', to try to get some distance from the atrocity. The result is, like much of Vonnegut's work, disturbing, humane and very funny.

WORKS TO READ

- *Cat's Cradle* (1963)
- *God Bless You, Mr Rosewater* (1965)
- *Slaughterhouse-Five* (1969)
- *Breakfast of Champions* (1973)
- *Deadeye Dick* (1982)

DID YOU KNOW?

Vonnegut made a cameo as himself in the 1986 US comedy *Back to School* (directed by Alan Metter) in which the lead character, Thornton Melon, hires Vonnegut to write an essay about Vonnegut's works. The final essay is however rejected by Thornton's tutor who says, 'Whoever did write it doesn't know the first thing about Kurt Vonnegut.'

Cat's Cradle, 1963

A minor character in *Slaughterhouse-Five* is the unsuccessful science-fiction writer Kilgore Trout, who had made his first appearance in *God Bless You, Mr Rosewater* (1965) and crops up again in *Breakfast of Champions* (1973) and elsewhere. Like Vonnegut, Trout imagines the world operating by different rules. It has been suggested that he is a sort of Vonnegut alter ego, in which case his utter failure as a novelist becomes a joke against Vonnegut himself; however, Vonnegut remarks that Trout is the only one of his characters with enough imagination to suspect that he might have been created by someone else.

Vonnegut's work was frequently banned or criticized in various communities across the US, but he remained an irrepressible advocate of free speech. As he himself might have said, so it goes. In writing books that dealt with serious subjects but could be enjoyed by the young, his aim was 'to catch people before they become generals and senators and presidents, and you poison their minds with humanity. Encourage them to make a better world.'

Vonnegut at home in New York in 1972

Any reviewer who expresses rage and loathing for a novel is preposterous. He or she is like a person who has put on full armor and attacked a hot fudge sundae.

VIRGINIA WOOLF

BRITISH

1882–1941

In early 1920 Virginia Woolf wrote happily that she had thought out an entirely new approach for her next novel: 'No scaffolding, scarcely a brick to be seen, all crepuscular, but the heart, the passion, humour, everything as bright as fire in the mist.' She was working on *Jacob's Room* (1922), but this innovative and experimental attitude permeates all her work.

Born into a literary family and educated at home while her brothers were sent to school and university, Woolf grew up with a passionate resentment of this discrimination; she became a Suffragist, Feminist and campaigner for women's education. 'A woman must have money and a room of her own if she is to write fiction,' she famously maintained in her extended essay *A Room of One's Own* (1929); she later blamed what she called 'the Angel in the House', an idealized image of domestic femininity, for obstructing women wanting to pursue careers as writers or in any of the professions. In her fiction, she focused on women's perceptions and experiences, rivalling James JOYCE in the bravura use of interior monologue and stream of consciousness.

These techniques reach a pinnacle in *Mrs Dalloway* (1925), which flows back and forth between a woman's thoughts on the day she is due to give a party and those of a shell-shocked young man approaching suicide. They are also seen in

WORKS TO READ

- *Mrs Dalloway* (1925)
- *To the Lighthouse* (1927)
- *Orlando* (1928)
- *A Room of One's Own* (1929)
- *The Collected Essays of Virginia Woolf* (2013)

DID YOU KNOW?

Artistic sisterly collaboration ensured many of Virginia Woolf's books were wrapped in dust jackets designed by her sister, the successful artist and designer Vanessa Bell. Virginia Woolf took much inspiration from her family, with the character of Mrs Dalloway based on Vanessa Bell – who, like Mrs Dalloway, found the prospect of hosting a party somewhat nervewracking.

A Room of One's Own, 1929

To the Lighthouse (1927) and *The Waves* (1931), both of which contain strong autobiographical elements. In the former, the sudden death of Mrs Ramsay and the self-pitying grief of her husband reflect Woolf's own experience of losing her mother; the latter mourns the premature death of her brother Thoby. More humorously, the mock biography *Orlando* (1928) – inspired by Woolf's intimacy with fellow writer Vita Sackville-West – features a central character who goes to bed one night a duke and wakes up a duchess; it is now a seminal text in gender studies.

In addition to being a novelist, Woolf was an indefatigable and sparkling letter-writer, diarist and essayist. The wit and sharp social observation of her work are often overlooked because of the emphasis placed on her mental instability. She suffered numerous nervous breakdowns and suicide attempts before finally, in the belief that she was definitely going mad, succeeding in taking her own life.

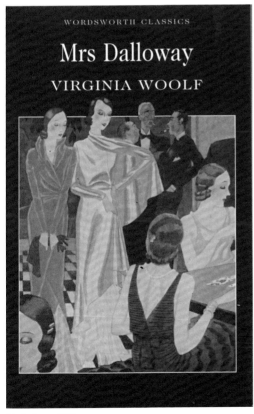

Mrs Dalloway, 1925

For most of history, Anonymous was a woman.

LU
_XUN

CHINESE
1881–1936

As a young medical student, Lu Xun was shown a photograph of a crowd of Chinese blankly and apathetically watching the execution of an accused spy. It was the formative moment of his career: he realized that if the people of his country were 'intellectually feeble', they would never become anything other than 'cannon fodder or gawping spectators'. He abandoned medicine in 1906 to become a writer. It was less important to him to improve the Chinese people's health than to reform their spirit.

Critical of the traditional Confucian thinking that dominated Chinese society, Lu Xun had already embraced Western culture and literature. As part of the New Culture Movement that emerged in China in the mid-1910s, he took to writing short stories in the vernacular, as opposed to Classical Chinese. His subjects were vernacular, too: poor, uneducated people living in small villages, drinking and gambling, and preoccupied with parochial concerns. Many of these stories are narrated with droll and sardonic detachment, but they are also savagely critical of the society they portray and of the narrow horizons and monstrous callousness of its people. His most famous character, the village handyman in *The Real Story of Ah-Q* (1921–2), is idle, belligerent, obsessed with his own status and generally despicable. When he is executed by firing squad, the watching crowd returns home disgruntled: 'the majority of them felt [it] wasn't a patch on decapitation.' Similar themes recur in his essays – notably

WORKS TO READ

- *Outcry* (1923)
- *Dawn Blossoms Plucked at Dusk* (essays, 1932)
- *Old Tales Retold* (short stories, 1935)
- *The Real Story of Ah-Q and Other Tales of China: The Complete Fiction of Lu Xun* (2009 edition)

DID YOU KNOW?

Lu Xun quit his teaching post at Zhongshan University after the Shanghai massacre of April 1927. He was considered for a Nobel Prize in Literature nomination later that year for *The Real Story of Ah-Q* but rejected the nomination as a protest against the political situation in China.

Dawn Blossoms Plucked at Dusk, 1932

There's no such thing as natural genius. I put my effort into work while others put theirs into drinking coffee.

Dawn Blossoms Plucked at Dusk (1932), based on his own early life – and in *Old Tales Retold* (1935), in which he gives a characteristically clear-sighted twist to traditional Chinese legends. Lu Xun's politics took a turn to the left in the early 1930s, but it was only after his death that he became a Communist icon. Mao Zedong adopted him as 'the saint of modern China' and praised his fight against 'the rotten society and the evil imperialist forces'. It's an attitude that would have surprised Lu Xun and that conveniently ignored his passionate support for exactly the sort of Western influence Mao sought to suppress.

Lu Xun remains a controversial figure in Chinese literature: though tourists flock to the park in Shanghai that bears his name and contains his tomb, he was always torn between a love of his country and a hatred for what it had done (under various regimes) to its people. He was, he wrote, 'as saddened by the miseries of [his characters] as I am infuriated by their reconciliation with their fate'.

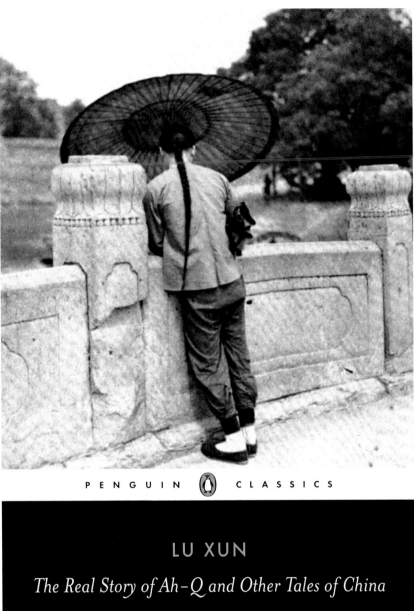

PENGUIN CLASSICS

LU XUN

The Real Story of Ah-Q and Other Tales of China

The Complete Fiction of Lu Xun

The Real Story of Ah-Q, 1921

STEFAN ZWEIG

AUSTRIAN

1881–1942

At the height of his fame, in the 1920s and 1930s, Stefan Zweig was one of the best-known and most widely translated authors in the world. He had also worked as a translator and written monographs on subjects as wide-ranging as Casanova, Balzac and Mary, Queen of Scots. By birth he was an Austro-Hungarian Jew; by inclination a pan-European, for whom watching the continent tearing itself apart, not once but twice in a generation, was a source of profound sorrow.

Born into a wealthy Viennese family, Zweig became a great documenter of the city's sparkling pre-World War I cultural milieu, where he portrayed passion and guilt lurking beneath surface respectability. By the end of the war, this world had collapsed and a deep nostalgia for it can be seen throughout his work.

In real life, as in his writings, Zweig was an observer: one commentator remarked that it is no coincidence he was living and working in the same city as Sigmund Freud. His narrators often seem cast adrift in a world too complicated for them to understand, most notably in his novel *Beware of Pity* (1939). Set tellingly in 1913, on the brink of war, it concerns a young cavalry officer who asks a woman to dance, unaware that she is lame. Visiting her family to apologize for his blunder, he is drawn into a web that centres on convincing the girl she can be cured: as the title suggests, only tragedy can result.

WORKS TO READ

- *Letter from an Unknown Woman* (novella, 1922)
- *Twenty-four Hours in the Life of a Woman* (novella, 1927)
- *Beware of Pity* (1939)
- *The Royal Game* (novella, 1941)
- *The World of Yesterday* (autobiography, 1942)

DID YOU KNOW?

When a new edition of Zweig's autobiography, *The World of Yesterday*, was reviewed unfavourably by Michael Hoffman of the *London Review of Books* in 2010 it created a significant backlash on the journal's Letters pages from disgruntled fans.

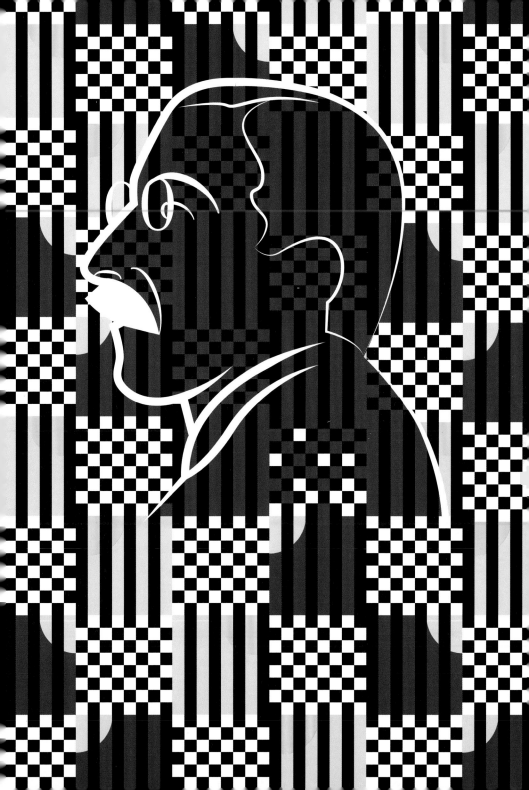

STEFAN ZWEIG
Schachnovelle

Beware of Pity was written in England, where Zweig and his wife moved in the 1930s to escape the spread of Nazism. From there they went to the US and finally to Brazil. These unsettled last years produced the acclaimed novella *The Royal Game* (1941), in which a chess game becomes an allegory for the battle between imagination and rigid totalitarian thinking, and the memoir *The World of Yesterday* (1942), which has been both praised for its portrayal of early 20th-century Vienna and criticized for revealing disappointingly little about the author himself. On the day the manuscript was sent to his publishers, Zweig and his wife committed suicide together. He left a note explaining that he could not face trying to rebuild his life 'after the world of my own language sank and was lost to me and my spiritual homeland, Europe, destroyed itself'.

Zweig on a voyage from New York to Brazil, date unknown

The Royal Game, 1941

GLOSSARY

absurdism The philosophy espoused by Albert Camus and Samuel Beckett, among others, that life has no inherent meaning or value. Camus maintained, however, that although we were doomed to disappointment if we sought meaning, we should continue to strive for it.

allegory A work in which the apparent meaning of the characters and events symbolizes something more philosophical, spiritual or political: in George Orwell's *Animal Farm*, for example, the animal characters represent specific political figures.

antihero A *protagonist* who lacks the traditional qualities and virtues – goodness, courage, honesty, etc. – of a hero.

autobiography The author's own life story, written by him- or herself.

belle époque (French: 'beautiful period') The period from the late 19th century until the beginning of World War I when life (for the wealthy) was settled and culturally rich.

bon mot (French: 'good word') A witticism, a clever and apt remark.

counter-culture A way of life that consciously rejects conventional social practices; often applied to the youthful drug-taking 'hippies' of the 1960s.

dystopia A nightmarish future society, often dominated by technology and/or a totalitarian government. Dystopias are represented in Aldous Huxley's *Brave New World* and George Orwell's *Nineteen Eighty-Four*.

Everyman An ordinary character, with no pretensions to conventional heroism.

existentialism A philosophy espoused by, among others, Simone de Beauvoir and Jean-Paul Sartre, which stresses the freedom of the human being and the belief that we are morally responsible for the choices we make.

imagery Figurative or descriptive language used to create visual or other sensory images in the reader's mind.

interior monologue A form of *stream of consciousness*, a way of expressing the thoughts and feelings of a character without the intervention of the author.

Kafkaesque Resembling the works of Franz Kafka – nightmarish, threatening, full of unanswered questions.

Lost Generation A generation that has lost a large number of its members in war and as a result has metaphorically lost its way and its values. The term is usually applied to the generation that grew to maturity during and immediately after World War I, and was used by American author Gertrude Stein (1874–1946) specifically to describe the young American writers she befriended in Paris in the 1920s (notably Ernest Hemingway and F Scott Fitzgerald).

magical (or magic) realism A style of narrative in which realistic elements are intertwined with the unrealistic in the form of magic, dreams and wild leaps of the imagination. Coined in Germany in the 1950s, it is now used particularly to describe the writings of South Americans such as Jorge Luis Borges and Gabriel García Márquez; it has also been applied to Italo Calvino, Angela Carter, Günter Grass and Salman Rushdie.

memoir A form of *autobiography* or biography, especially one written from personal knowledge and often focusing on a particular aspect or period of the subject's life.

metaphor A figure of speech making an implied comparison, applying a description imaginatively to something to which it is not connected literally ('pearls of wisdom', 'all the world's a stage').

modernism In literature, a form of writing that moved away from 19th-century traditions of storytelling to experiment with such concepts as *non-linear* narrative and *stream of consciousness*. The term is often applied to the works of T S ELIOT, James JOYCE and Virginia WOOLF.

monograph An essay or other short work on a single subject or aspect of a subject.

non-linear A narrative, not told in the usual straightforward manner in which each event follows logically and chronologically from the one before. This may involve beginning in the middle or at the end of a story and telling it in flashback; shifting backwards and forwards in time; developing two or more stories side by side; using more than one viewpoint, and other such devices. Non-linear narratives are a feature of the work of William FAULKNER and Kurt VONNEGUT, among many others.

pastiche A work, often comical or satirical, composed in the style of another: Graham GREENE's *Monsignor Quixote* is a pastiche of Cervantes' *Don Quixote*.

picaresque From the Spanish *picaro* meaning a rascal, a picaresque novel depicts a roguish hero's adventures through loosely connected episodes.

postmodernism A late 20th-century reaction against *modernism* which in literature tends to feature a self-conscious awareness on the part of the author that he or she is writing a work of fiction.

protagonist A central character, whether heroic or otherwise.

realism A style of writing that rejects idealism and romanticism in favour of the unadorned, often painful treatment of daily life, particularly among the unwealthy and unaristocratic.

science fiction A genre of fiction involving imagined scientific changes (often time travel or travel to other worlds) some time in the future; extended to include imagined social, environmental and other changes.

speculative fiction Any fiction which 'speculates' on, for example, how certain aspects of society will be in the future, or might be if a historical event had turned out a different way. The term can encompass *science fiction*, fantasy and many other genres.

stream of consciousness A literary style brought to prominence by James JOYCE, Marcel PROUST and Virginia WOOLF, whereby a character's thoughts and feelings flow without interruption.

symbolism An artistic and literary movement that uses symbols rather than direct statements to suggest or evoke emotions and express ideas.

tetralogy See *trilogy*.

trilogy A set of three linked novels or other works, often featuring successive generations of the same family. When a fourth book is added, it becomes a *tetralogy*.

unreliable narrator A narrator whose opinions and feelings the reader cannot trust. This may be because the narrator is young and/or disturbed (as in J D SALINGER's *The Catcher in the Rye*), emotionally involved in the events he or she is recounting (Ford Madox FORD's *The Good Soldier*) or a criminal or malefactor (some modern detective stories and thrillers). It's a device that forces readers to judge for themselves what is in the author's mind.

vernacular The language of a particular country or social group, previously referred to as the 'folksy', day-to-day speech of uneducated people, as in Chinua ACHEBE's *Things Fall Apart* and Zora Neale HURSTON's *Their Eyes Were Watching God*.

INDEX

INDEX

PICTURE CREDITS

akg-images Fototeca Gilardi 140. **Alamy** Everett Collection Historical 105; Everett Historical Collection 100; Geraint Lewis 32; Granger Historical Archive 60, 168, 200; Granger Historical Picture Archive, illustration by Vanessa Bell 208; Heritage Image Partnership Ltd. 181; Keystone Pictures USA 12; MGM/Moviestore Collection 193; Pictorial Press Ltd 69; Rod Collins 57; The Art Archive/Bibliotheque Nationale, Paris 172; Trinity Mirror/Mirrorpix 124; World History Archive 133. **Bridgeman Images** 25; Archives Charmet 141, 185; Christie's Images 144, 160; Rene Saint Paul 44. **Getty Images** Alfred Eisenstaedt/The LIFE Picture Collection 93; Apic 188; Bettmann 65, 113, 149; Evening Standard 80; Gamma-Keystone via Getty Images 29; Gene Lester 16; Horacio Villalobos/Corbis via Getty Images 36; Horst Tappe/Pix Inc./The LIFE Images Collection 157; Hulton Archive 120; Jack Mitchell 153; Lipnitzki/Roger Viollet/Getty Images 33; Peter Stackpole/The LIFE Picture Collection 88; Santi Visalli 205; Ullstein Bild via Getty Images 217. **Photoshot** Idols 56. **REX Shutterstock** Columbia/Merchant Ivory 108; ITV 76; Kobal Collection/20th Century Fox 64; Sutton-Hibbert 20. **TopFoto** Keystone 180; ullsteinbild 96.

We would like to acknowledge and thank the following publishers and companies for their kind help in the making of this book. Every effort has been made to contact copyright holders. We apologise if any omissions have been made been.

Argo (1954) 196. **Bloomsbury Publishing Plc.** 21. **Faber & Faber** 48, 49, 61, 109, photo by Alamy/sjbooks 77. **Fischer Taschenbuch** 216. **Reprinted by permission of HarperCollins Publishers Ltd.** 101, 125. **Houghton Mifflin Harcourt**, Orlando: Harcourt (1998) 41. **Indian Thought Publications** 164. **Metro Fifth Avenue Press LLC** 212. **New Directions Publishing** 128. **Reproduced by permission of Penguin Books Ltd.** 24, 68, 89, 97, 112, 121, 129, 132, 169, 201, 204, 213; Illustration by Peter Goodfellow 37; photo by Alamy/Granger Historical Archive, illustration by Elmer Hader 192; photo by Alamy/JHPhoto 116; photo by Alamy/sjbooks 45, 161. **Penguin Random House Grupo Editorial**, illustration by Jordi Sàbat 145. **Penguin Random House LLC** 17; photo by Alamy/Jonny White 13. **Penguin Random House UK** 28, 40, 52, 136, 148, 156, 176; Photo by Bridgeman Images/Christie's Images/Art by Leslie C. Holland 104. **Pocket Books (Mm)** 152. **Prentice Hall** 184. **Steidl** photo by Getty Images/Sean Gallup 85. **Stellar Books** 92. **The American University in Cairo Press** 137. **Wordsworth Editions Ltd.** 72, 209. **YMCA Press**, photo by Bridgeman Images/Tobie Mathew Collection 189.

ACKNOWLEDGEMENTS

Well, I've got to the part of the book where all those that made it possible should be thanked and I cannot think of an angle. What would a writer do? Should I pack my bags, hole up in a cottage in the Orkney Islands and re-centre my mind whilst getting closer to nature and wondering at the vast expanse of the sea? I may have problems maintaining my school run responsibilities from there, so I think it might be better to get on with it here.

Firstly, it's a pleasure to thank the delightful Caroline Taggart. Incidentally, I possessed a couple of her books on grammar already, so I was genuinely thrilled when she accepted the offer to write the book even if I was also a little anxious about the correct use of 'me' and 'I' in my emails. I needn't have worried as it's all there in her books.

Thanks to Hannah Knowles, my brilliant Commissioning Editor, for once again having the faith in me to produce another book. It seems I must be doing something right. Good luck with your next role and I hope we get to work together again.

To Pauline Bache, my Editor, who has the patience of a saint coupled with a steely resolve to make sure design and illustrations were in on time, thank you.

Thanks also to Giulia Hetherington, Picture Researcher, as this particular project was extremely difficult to resolve and track down rights for. And Jack Storey and Meskerem Berhane for guiding us all effortlessly through production.

My wife, Olivia Tuohy, who has perfected the glowering look rising from behind her laptop, that indicates that I am not the only one who has work to do when, once again, I interrupt her workflow to ask her opinion on an illustration. An opinion I might add that is always on the nail.

And let's hear it for all those second hand bookshops out there, in particular the fantastic Demelza bookshop in Hythe which supplied me with a large number of books for invaluable research purposes. I've got a few to get through, still.

Thank you to everyone. Books may only have the names of one or two people on their covers but they only exist because of the hard dedication of many more than that.